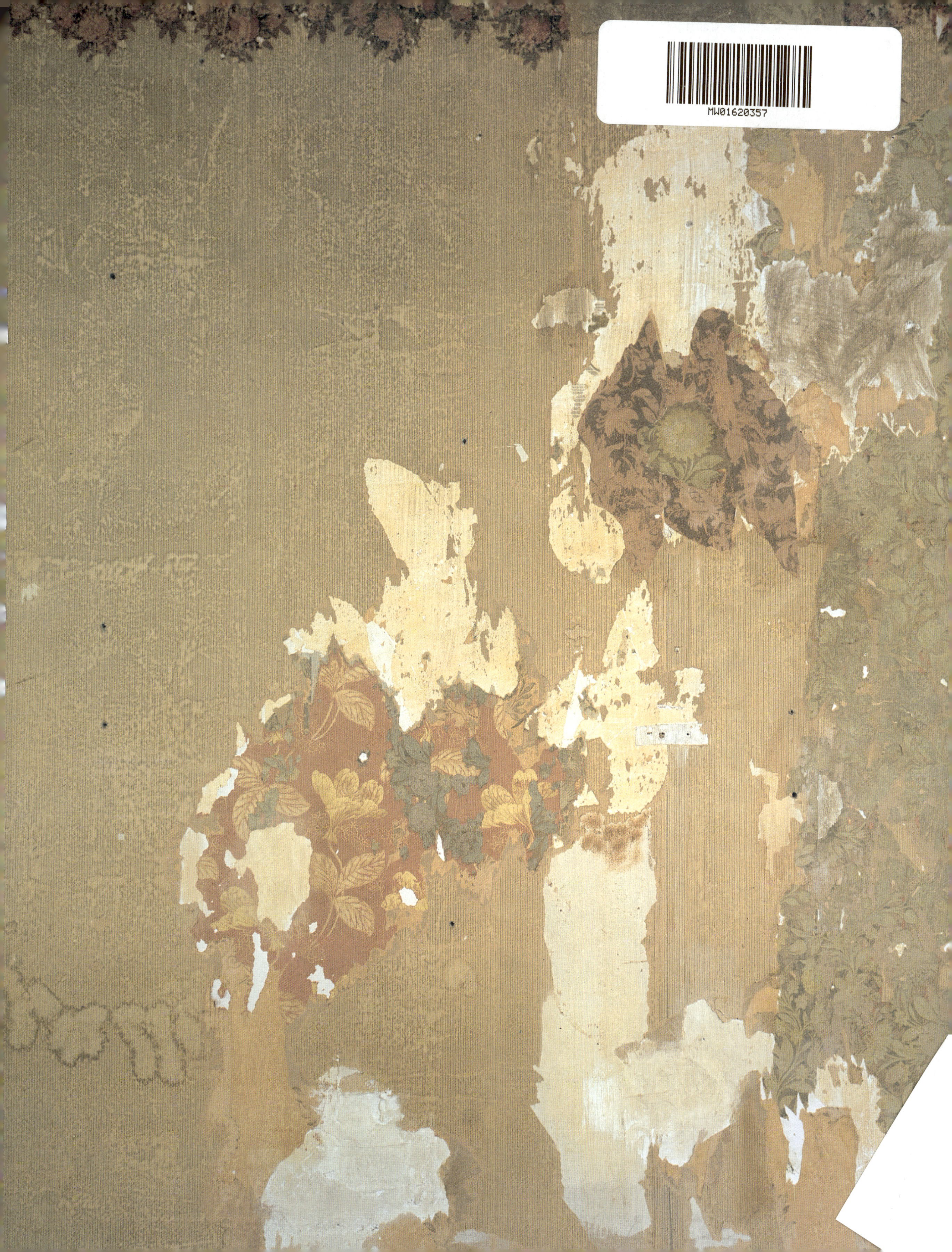

HARUMI KLOSSOWSKA DE ROLA

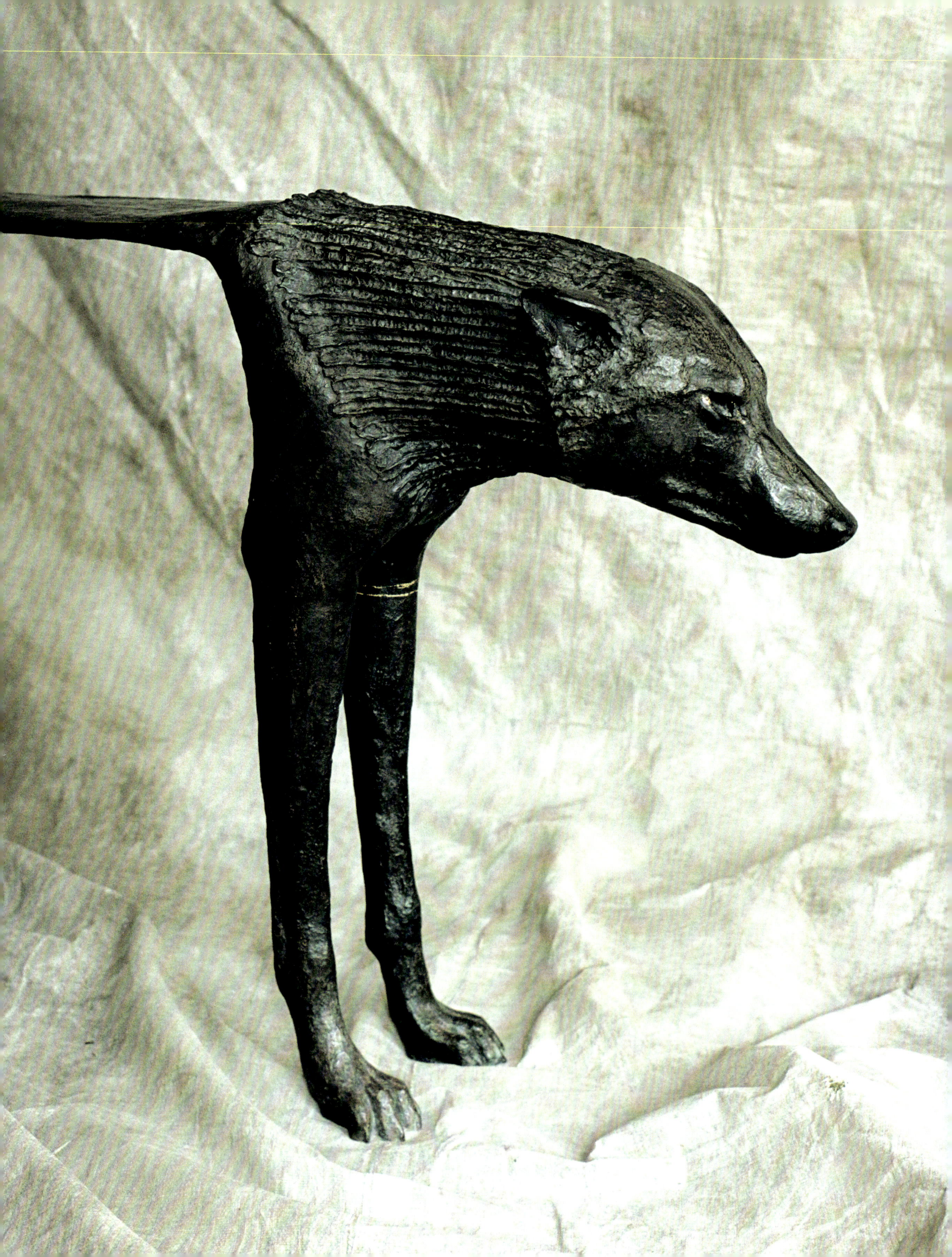

HARUMI KLOSSOWSKA DE ROLA

Sacred Woods

ESSAY BY

OLIVIER BERGGRUEN

WITH PHOTOGRAPHS BY

ADRIEN DIRAND

ACQUAVELLA

RIZZOLI
NEW YORK

This publication accompanies the exhibition

HARUMI KLOSSOWSKA DE ROLA

Sacred Woods

ON VIEW

January 11–February 23, 2025
Acquavella Palm Beach
340 Royal Poinciana Way, Suite M309
Palm Beach, FL 33480

All photos by Adrien Dirand

ISBN 978-0-8478-7585-6
Library of Congress Control Number: 2024951779

DISTRIBUTION

Rizzoli International Publications, Inc.
49 West 27th Street
New York, NY 10001
www.rizzoliusa.com

DESIGN

HvADesign, NY

PRINT

O.G.M. SpA, Italy

Front cover: *Lakshmi,* 2022 (see p. 106)
Frontispiece: *Wepwawet,* 2022 (detail) (see p. 100)

TABLE OF CONTENTS

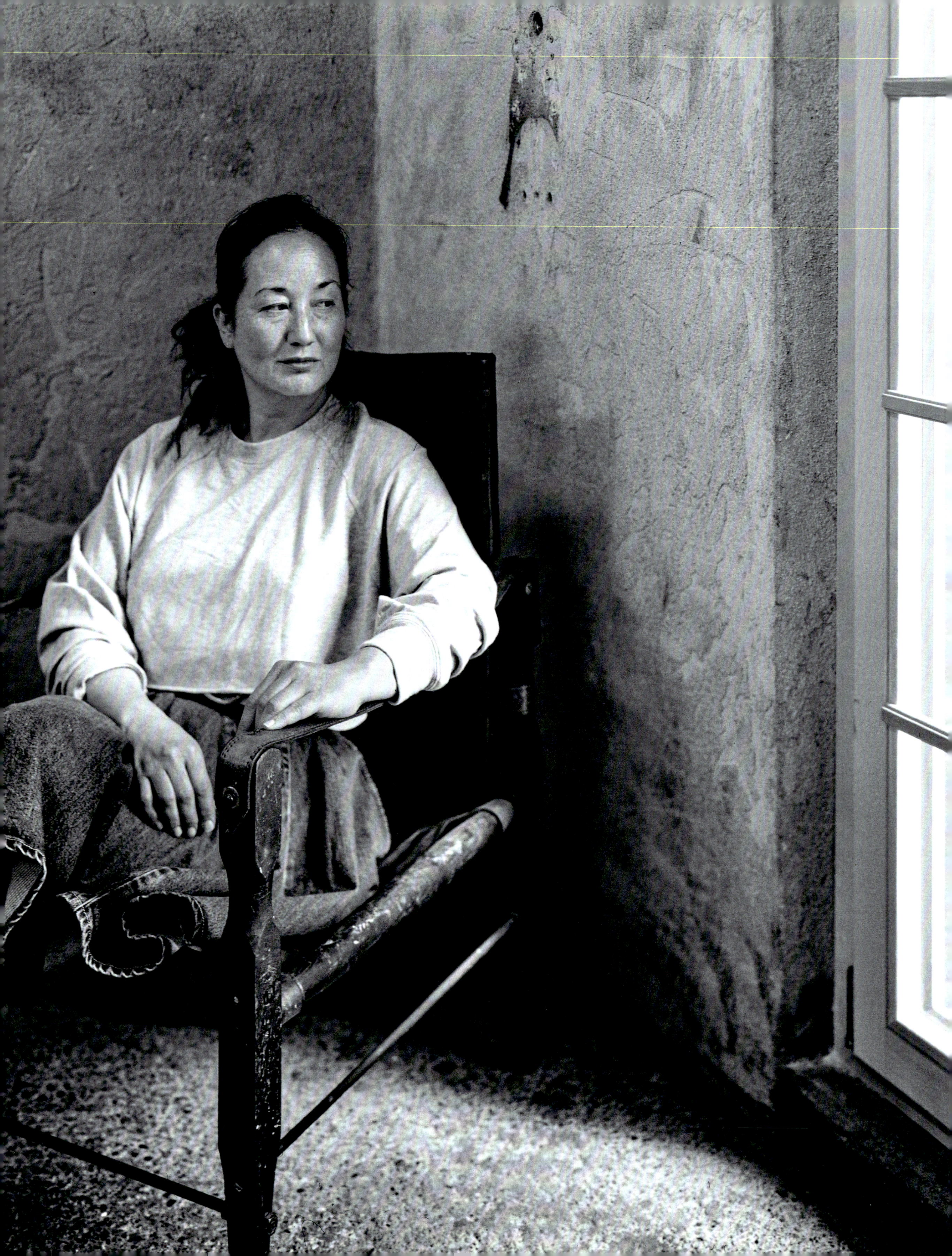

INTRODUCTION

We are delighted to present our first exhibition with the Swiss-based artist Harumi Klossowska de Rola, which will be on view in our Palm Beach gallery from January 11 – February 23, 2025.

Titled *Sacred Woods,* the exhibition features new and recent sculptures that explore the artist's reverential fascination with the beauty of the untamed natural world. Inspired by the grace and majesty of the animal kingdom, the show includes over a dozen sensitively rendered animals crafted out of bronze, alabaster, or wood; each is ennobled with a sense of spirit, physicality, and emotion. Her sentient sculptures function as living, totemic entities, creating a bridge between nature and humankind.

The artist explains her desire to connect people to the natural world and our environment:

> "*My main inspiration is about wild animals, or plants or trees; they're not domesticated in my work. I look through my mother's eyes, through animism.... Nature is cruel, but we've utterly separated ourselves from the natural world, where we were surrounded by species more powerful than ours. It's important for us today to get reacquainted with nature and with fear, to help make us aware that animals are just as important as we are.*"

The passage of time and a rich sense of history is integral to Harumi's work; her hand-crafted sculptures incorporate materials layered with age and history, embracing how mediums such as bronze will evolve and oxidize over time. With an exquisite attention to detail and surface, they feature rich patinas, often highlighted with passages of gold leaf. Each sculpture begins with extensive preparatory drawings and modeling before the artist arrives at the final form. To make her sculptures, Harumi collaborates closely with skilled foundry artisans, often at the Fonderie de Coubertin in Saint-Rémy-lès-Chevreuse or at the Fonderie Patrick Laroche in Paris. Harumi's command of material and her keen attention to detail across her artistic practice is evident in each object she creates.

Drawing inspiration from a wide range of sources, the artist's practice is informed by an array of cultures and aesthetic traditions, from Ancient Egyptian, Greek, and Roman mythology to Art Nouveau and Romanticism and Japanese Shintoism and the aesthetic of wabi-sabi. Harumi's studio practice is equally influenced by her personal history and environment. Residing and working on the property of her childhood home, located in the town of Rossinière in the Swiss Alps, the artist has kept a dialogue with the nature and woods that surround her home. Her sculptures combine inspiration from the wild animals inhabiting these forests with historical and mythical creatures from ancient cultures and civilizations. As Harumi explains, "The link between us and nature has been sort of fading away in this last century. I'm trying to reconcile it.... My whole approach has been how to reconnect people with our old soul."

For their work on this exhibition and catalogue, we would like to acknowledge and thank the following people. Our gratitude goes to the photographer Adrien Dirand, who so beautifully captured the images of Harumi's work and her world at Rossinière; he was instrumental not only in photographing her work but also in bringing this book to life. We would like also thank Olivier Berggruen for his insightful essay on Harumi's work, which eloquently explores the complex and wide range of influences that inspire the artist's practice and her meticulous dedication to craft and beauty in making her sculptures.

We would like to also thank our graphic designer Henk van Assen and Melissa Leone at HvADesign and Giuseppina Leone and the team at OGM for working together on the design and production of this publication. Our thanks also go to Charles Miers and Ellen Cohen at Rizzoli International Publications for partnering with us on the book's distribution. At the gallery, we would like to acknowledge Hannah Honan and Emily Crowley, who worked closely with the studio on the show, and also Molly Aubry, Jean Edmonson, and Eric Theriault.

Finally, our sincere gratitude goes to Harumi and her studio manager, Khalil Outassou, for collaborating with us on the many facets of this exhibition. Above all, we would like to thank Harumi for making these beautiful works.

—ELEANOR ACQUAVELLA

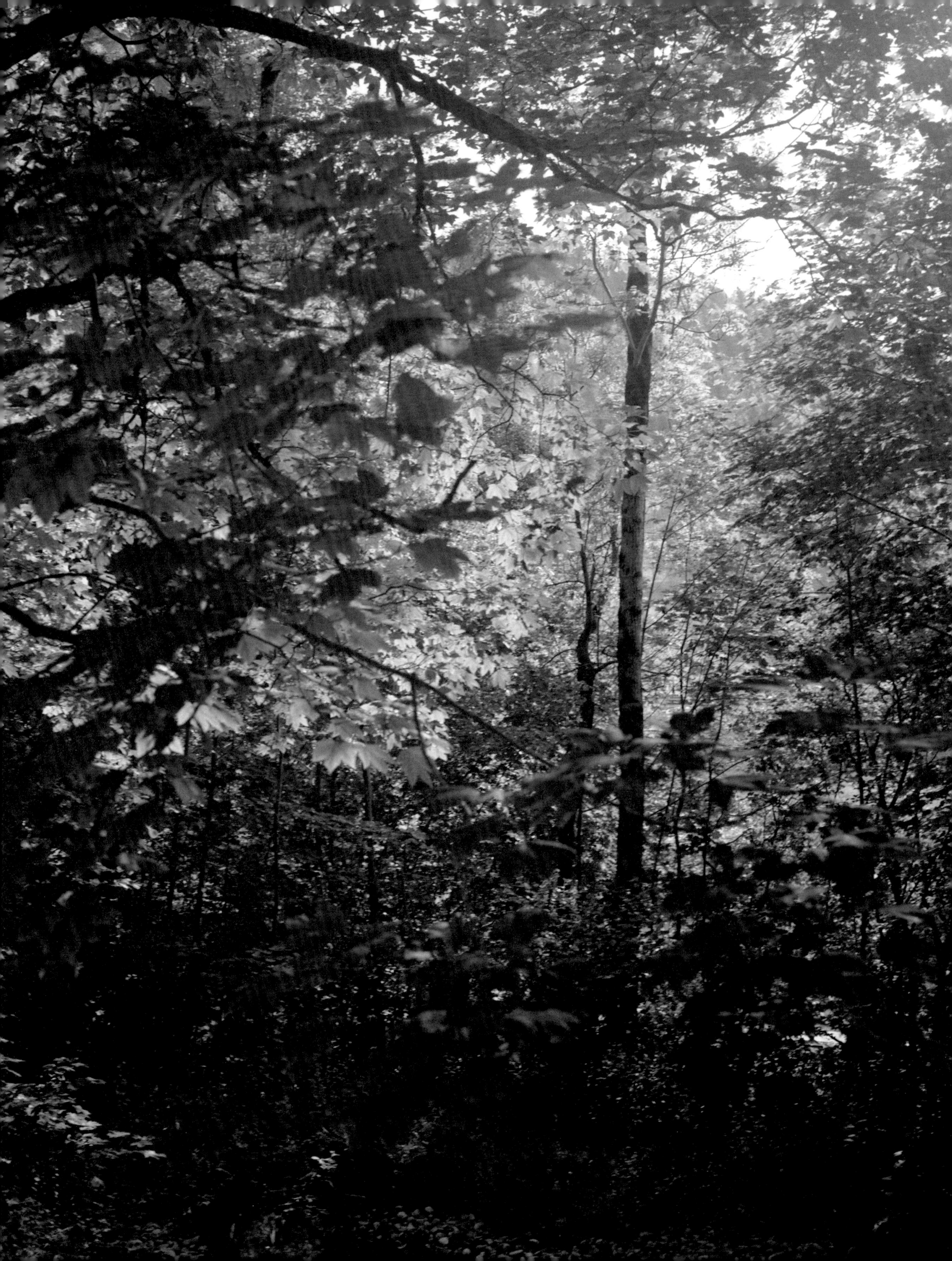

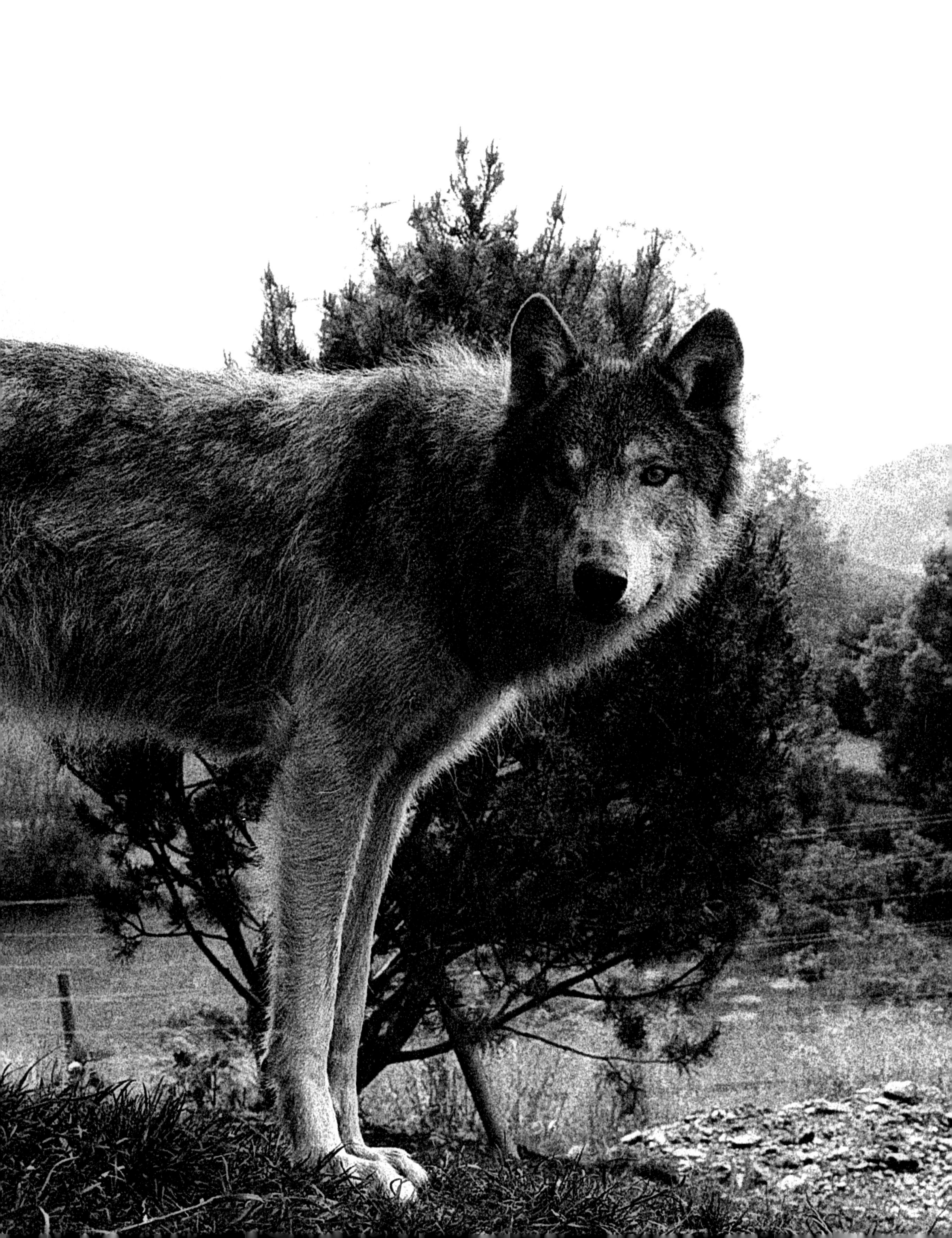

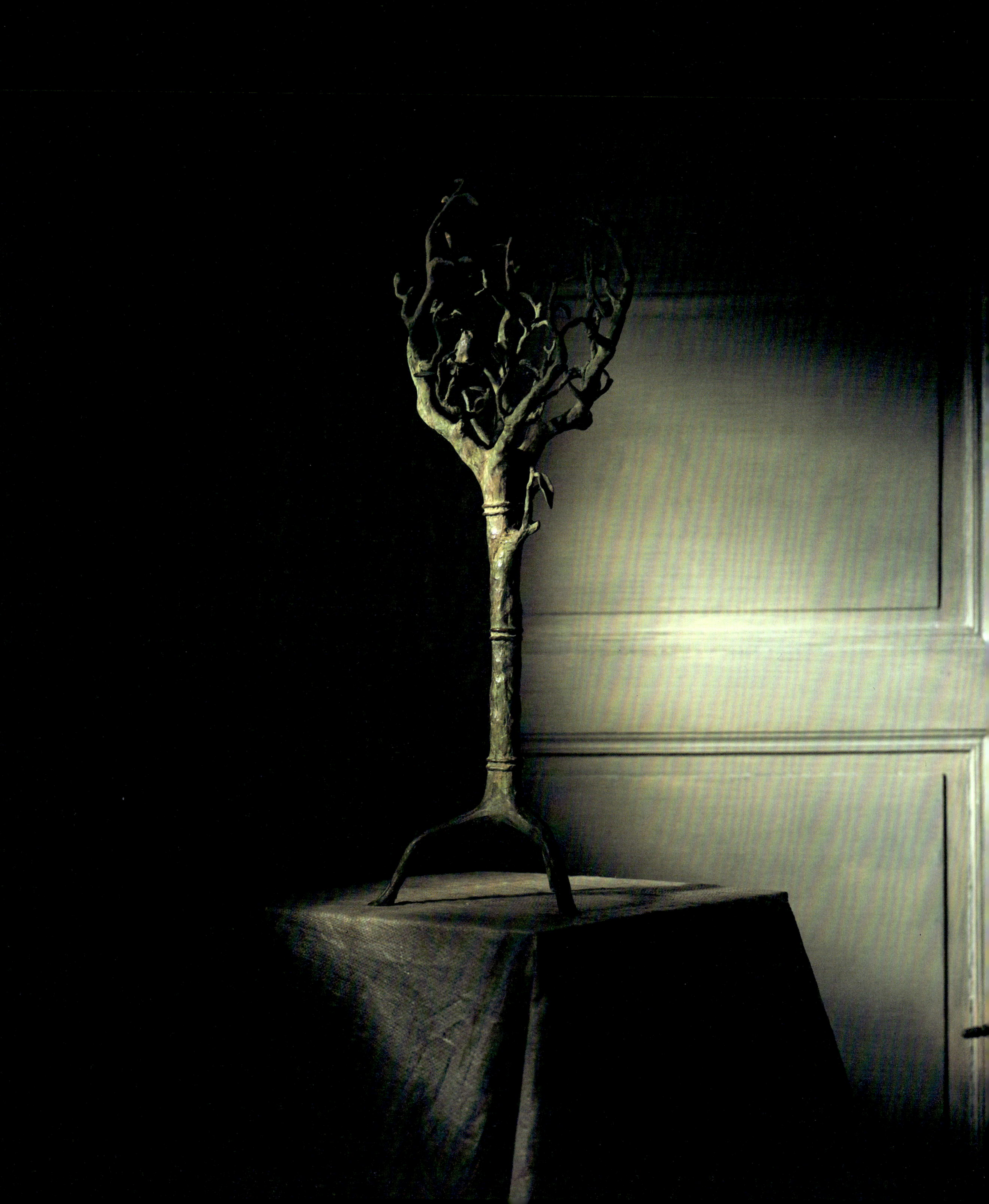

OLIVIER BERGGRUEN

SCULPTURE, EXTENDED

ITINERARIES

Harumi grew up near Gruyères in Switzerland, surrounded by misty mountains and cerulean skies, waking up to the sounds of cowbells and French being spoken in slow cadences. Both her parents were artists, a father of Polish-French extraction and a Japanese mother; despite their different backgrounds, they shared traditional notions of craftsmanship that also reflected ethical and spiritual preoccupations, since their artistic practices were always tethered to a quest for the essence of life, that which makes it meaningful and worthwhile.

In his pursuit of art, Harumi's father, the painter Balthus, cultivated a taste for the esoteric, invoking the transubstantiation of materials and colors in quasimystical terms; in his studio he would spend countless hours grinding colors from precious materials such as lapis lazuli, using secret formulas from ancient times that could transform the painting into a revelation, somewhat like alchemy. As for Setsuko, Harumi's mother, she would create ceramics and paintings that adhered to ideals of formal beauty as defined by traditional Japanese aesthetics.

In the famous *In Praise of Shadows* by Jun'ichiro Tañizaki (1933)[1], the author's absorption in the world at hand reveals an aesthetic attitude, which shows reverence for everyday situations and objects. Rather than clarity and light that characterizes much Western art, Tanizaki praises a certain effacement, ambiguity, and subtlety, paying closer attention to the refined tones of shadows reflected by subtle materials such as gold (in the form of embroidery), lacquers, or even certain stones and crystals. He prefers those withered, subtle patinas of the East to the polished and shiny silverware and flashy surfaces of the West. His treatise is divided into multiple sections, where subjects as diverse as traditional craftsmanship, the art of lacquer (and the way it is perceived when lit by a candle), the "just" contemplation of the moon and the stars, the geishas glimpsed in the half-light of a brothel, etc. In Japan, this feeling of reverence for transient things is called *mono no aware*. The cult of the ephemeral—empathy for things with no intrinsic value, and no desire to possess them—implies a kind of "phenomenalism":

a sense that the world is intangibly abundant; its multiplicity, its daily beauty evokes an appreciation for the inherent riches hidden beneath the surface. As it draws our attention to that which is particular, this phenomenalism emphasizes a variety of situations for us to contemplate, and the need to resist the temptation to essentialize borrowed concepts such as beauty, what's real, or sublime.

Naturally, these influences from her family shaped Harumi's artistic training and outlook. In her early twenties, she started experimenting with rare materials and stones. As a first step, she brought together exquisitely crafted Chinese buttons, semiprecious stones, and textiles, weaving shimmering surfaces of dense layers and materials; then she embarked on jewelry design thanks to a commission by Boucheron for its one hundred and fiftieth anniversary; there were more collaborations using stones and bronze for Chopard. After seeing the work of Claude and François-Xavier Lalanne in Paris, Harumi started working on bronze sculptures, a process that involved producing drawings and small sized maquettes as blueprints for the finished works. More recently, a series of private commissions and exhibitions (including one for Valentino in Paris), steered her work towards the use of bronze in larger sculptures of animal motifs. Nowadays, the majority of her works are fabricated at the Fonderie de Coubertin in Saint-Rémy-lès-Chevreuse near Paris.

EGYPT REIMAGINED

Let us picture Egypt in ancient times: vast regions with nothing but the sun burning high up in the sky; and then, through human intervention, came this imposing architecture where hieratic buildings and funerary monuments are adorned with sacred animals and other mythical creatures, effigies of kings and queens. At night, the movement of stars feels eerily palpable. The architecture of the ancient funerary monument reveals a quest for proportions in which human beings are able to establish a convincing relationship with the immensity of the landscape; furthermore, a secret numerology seems to govern the way in which these monuments were built. This may have appealed to Harumi's reverence for the esoteric.

Daily rituals would celebrate the victory of the sun over darkness—funerary monuments offer us depictions of Apophis being threatened by Re's warriors. When we look at Harumi's silent, impassible animals sculpted in bronze, a similar spirit seems to animate them. It is a silent gaze. These animals are hybrid in a sense: they are sentient beings, fantastical, noble, stoic in the vastness of the desert and life's ebbs and flows. They both belong to the realm of nature and also outgrow and extend beyond their natural condition. Harumi imagines new possibilities for their beings; they are powerful and mature, as though such attributes could accommodate other lives, words, signs.

If Ancient Egypt emphasized symbolic and mythical forms of thought, in the modern world such expressions of the magical link between human beings and the natural realm are no longer in fashion. They have been replaced by scientific belief. Yet for centuries, various living creatures have been revered as quasidivine symbols of nature. The animals Harumi creates can be seen as symbols of irrational forces. They are part of a more general process of the pagan worship of nature that is common in many ancestral belief systems.

A cursory study of Pharaonic Egypt reveals ancient rites that conferred upon nature—plants, stones, and living creatures—a magical and supernatural character. In Ancient Egypt, nature assumes a sacred character because it represents the eternal forces of the universe. The gods take the shape of sacred symbols with powers to dispel bad spirits, while animals are intermediaries between human beings and supernatural forces. Divine invocation is thought to be a way of influencing demigods. In one of the works in the exhibition, a pair of serpents traces a fluid and slender line in space, while their gaze is strangely self-absorbed, as if to suggest that they behold magical powers. In the *Book of the Dead*, the serpent Apophis represents the forces of darkness and assumes a malevolent role by trying to prevent the sun's progress. Ancient Egyptians held the belief that a sense of order—the daily victory of the sun over darkness—could be maintained through rituals directed against Apophis; in funerary texts it is quite common to find depictions of Apophis being threatened by Re's warriors. In *Serpentes*, Harumi's simplicity of form, with its emphasis on elongated biomorphism and fragments of a poetic shorthand, bears witness to this influence.

THE REALM OF NATURE

Since the heyday of Romanticism, artists never stopped proclaiming their desire to be in communion with nature. After a trip to Egypt in 1929, Paul Klee said to his students: "The artist is a human being, himself nature and a part of the realm of nature." Thus, the feeling of being at one with nature was born out of the "discovery of unsuspected relations from one element to another."[2] Like Klee and generations of artists before her, Harumi has assembled a collection of natural history specimens—herbs, leaves, flowers, algae, moss, butterflies, frogs, stones, and crystals—studying their color, shape, and structure. She has also marveled at various plants or fruits in order to learn about their internal structure. The vein of a leaf; the grooves of tree bark; a snail's shell: this vast dictionary of forms can be reproduced with intention, providing a model of artistic creation, one that could be manipulated through growth, repetition, and extension.

In 1753, William Hogarth published *The Analysis of Beauty*, a book where he formulates his conception of the visual arts. Hogarth conceives of a morphology of how one perceives natural sights, objects, and artifacts; at the most basic level, forms are governed by a serpentine "line of beauty." Artistic language is modeled on the language of nature. *The Analysis of Beauty* renders the world more intelligible, giving it an aesthetic dimension of which the serpentine line embodies liveliness and a sense of movement.

Harumi is familiar with such notions of beauty that stem from nature; yet she is keenly aware that the practice of applied arts to which she is devoted also involves a process of stylization, in which the natural world is abstracted; particular elements are idealized, while others are dismissed. This process is arbitrary and requires considerable skill and imagination in equal measure.

Harumi's creations display flat decorative surfaces, yet these are not devoid of a sense of armature, as in the fine, shimmering colors of her jewelry inspired by butterflies, dragonflies, eagles, serpents—a whole language rooted in the natural world. Forms are suspended somewhere between solidity and lightness, surface and depth, curvature and angles. These works testify to Harumi's natural affinity with aestheticism. They stress harmony, balance, texture, equilibrium, patterns, and surfaces. At times we are reminded of Japanese ukiyo-e prints where the emphasis was on diagonals, perspective, and asymmetry.

Her objects carry a sense of proportion and texture that is refined yet allow for elements of subversion, as in her bronze sculptures which take inspiration from Egyptian deities. Here, playing with the rules releases a sense of elasticity, introducing hints of distortion, as in the elongated seats and benches that are adorned with effigies of Sekhmet and Mafdet. In one of his notebooks, published under the title *Culture and Value,* Ludwig Wittgenstein wrote: "A beautiful garment that is transformed (coagulates, as it were) into worms and serpents if its wearer looks smugly at himself in the mirror."[3] In Harumi's case, the worms and serpents have indeed become beautiful, their sweeping lines and arabesques transforming the surrounding space by giving the natural realm a more poetic, sumptuous expression. In contrast to Wittgenstein's aphorism, this mirror reflects the beauty of worms, serpents, and the enchanted world to which Harumi has given a palpable presence.

GENEALOGIES

Apart from the influence her parents exerted on her early on in life, we could easily establish a catalog of Harumi's references, artists she admires: Diego Giacometti, whose furniture in bronze is adorned with wild animals such as the ones he encountered in his youth in the remote Val Bregaglia, or Claude and François-Xavier Lalanne, whose practice using a variety of materials ranging from electroplated metals to bronze and textiles, conciliates a formal language inherited from Art Nouveau with a Surrealist state of mind. It is worth noting that Antoinette de Watteville, the mother of her brothers Thadée and Stanislas, lived on the shores of Lake Geneva in a house furnished by Giacometti. Harumi's meditations on animalism owe much to the writings of Barry Lopez, ranging from *Arctic Dreams, Imagination and Desire in a Northern Landscape* (1986) to *Embrace Fearlessly the Burning World* (2022), in which the American essayist examines the relation between humans and nature in faraway lands, particularly the moment of confrontation between animals and persons. In his ecological preoccupations, Lopez sometimes tends to romanticize nature. This somehow suits Harumi, who claims for herself the Romantic dream of being at one with the natural world. In another book, *Of Wolves and Men* (1978), Lopez emphasizes the crucial moment of the exchange of gazes. Harumi offers only the most cursory depiction of animals' eyes, yet she is able to portray the noble, dignified nature of these creatures, infusing them with sentience.

At the dawn of the modern era, when the Industrial Revolution spread from Britain to the rest of Europe, a newly found kinship with the cosmos emerged, through the idea of the noble savage, the quasimythical creature extolled by Jean-Jacques Rousseau, or with the early German Romantic poetry of Novalis and Friedrich Hölderlin, in which the union between the sky, woods, birds, and the sea would be celebrated, where humans were once again attuned to the environment. This was the world of Johann Wolfgang von Goethe, Alexander von Humboldt, Henry David Thoreau, Gerard Manley Hopkins, and John Muir. If the development of modern science pushed civilization towards annihilation and mechanization, it also gave humankind a renewed sense of connection with nature—between natural and animal forms, landscape and nature, and other forms of enchantment that resonate more with art and poetry. Being in awe of nature, this interest in observing natural phenomena also involves time: the notion of the flow of things, found in Heraclitus, the change of seasons: growth, development, extinction, regeneration.

Other sources of inspiration that Harumi acknowledges include the animist traditions of Japan, in which animals are imbued with magical powers; these took hold during the young artist's trips to Japan, where she was deeply impressed by craftsmanship from the Kyoto school, and in particular by the craft of the Mingei artist Kawai Kanjirō. Kanjirō was a master in the art of glazing ceramics, ranging from red copper to brown iron and cobalt—but first and foremost, a teacher in humility, perseverance and absorption into one's craft.

CRAFTING, MAKING

The Romantics celebrated inspiration, creativity, imagination, and expression, preferring the freedom of individuality over the weight of constricting traditions. At the end of the eighteenth century, Jacques-Louis David held the conventions of artistic education responsible for the decline of the arts, while Joshua Reynolds proclaimed that it was necessary to relearn the craft of painting away from stifling rules. For his part, Philipp Otto Runge declared that in order to succeed, we have to become like children again. Could the artist reach a state of innocence and purity so as to give an unmediated image of the world, by turning his/her back on academic rules?

You could also make the opposite argument, that knowing the rules can help the artist reach greater freedom; by learning a craft (working consistently with bronze, wood and precious stones, in the case of Harumi), one gains the ability to outgrow tradition, precisely because one is familiar with it. In other words, mastering a craft precludes one from the risk of being accused of doing one's job badly. Artisanal work implies the observance and interpretation of certain rules; its success is partly linked to the work being deemed correct, without having to be accurate or conforming to a preexisting model. By mastering their craft, the artist gains greater freedom and the strength to be transgressive. This is the notion of métier, of humility, reverence in the face of craft; from this perspective, mastery is no longer starkly opposed to inspiration and originality.

Furthermore, we can ask the question, under what circumstances does craft become art? Where do we draw the line between these two realms? And how fluid are they? Instead of this age-old question, perhaps we should ask how the notion of craft, with its own rules, can lead to openness, freedom, to deliberate gestures and configurations that are unexpected. If these rules are open-ended, leading to new experiments, then we can imagine how a discipline as storied and codified as sculpture can outgrow its traditional definition and function, stretching, reinventing, taking itself apart, but more than anything else, stripping itself down to its bare essentials. Here I think it is important to dispel the notion that Harumi's practice is primarily ornamental, although she began as a jewelry designer; her vocabulary stresses graphic marks indebted to certain archetypes. Forms become emblematic of the spirit of the world of flora and fauna. The persistence of memory leads to a reevaluation of formal language, stretched in ways that are unexpected, yet imbued with a truth which is that of the artist.

—OLIVIER BERGGRUEN, OCTOBER 2024

I wish to thank Harumi Klossowska de Rola for her generous welcome in Switzerland, and Mebrak Tareke and Tobias Berggruen for their editorial suggestions.

NOTES

1
Jun'ichirō Tanizaki, *In Praise of Shadows* (New York: Vintage, 2019).

2
René Crevel, *Paul Klee* (Paris: Gallimard, 1930), 10.

3
Ludwig Wittgenstein, *Culture and Value,* G. H. von Wright with Heikki Nyman, eds., Peter Winch, tr. (Oxford: Basil Blackwell, 1980), 22e.

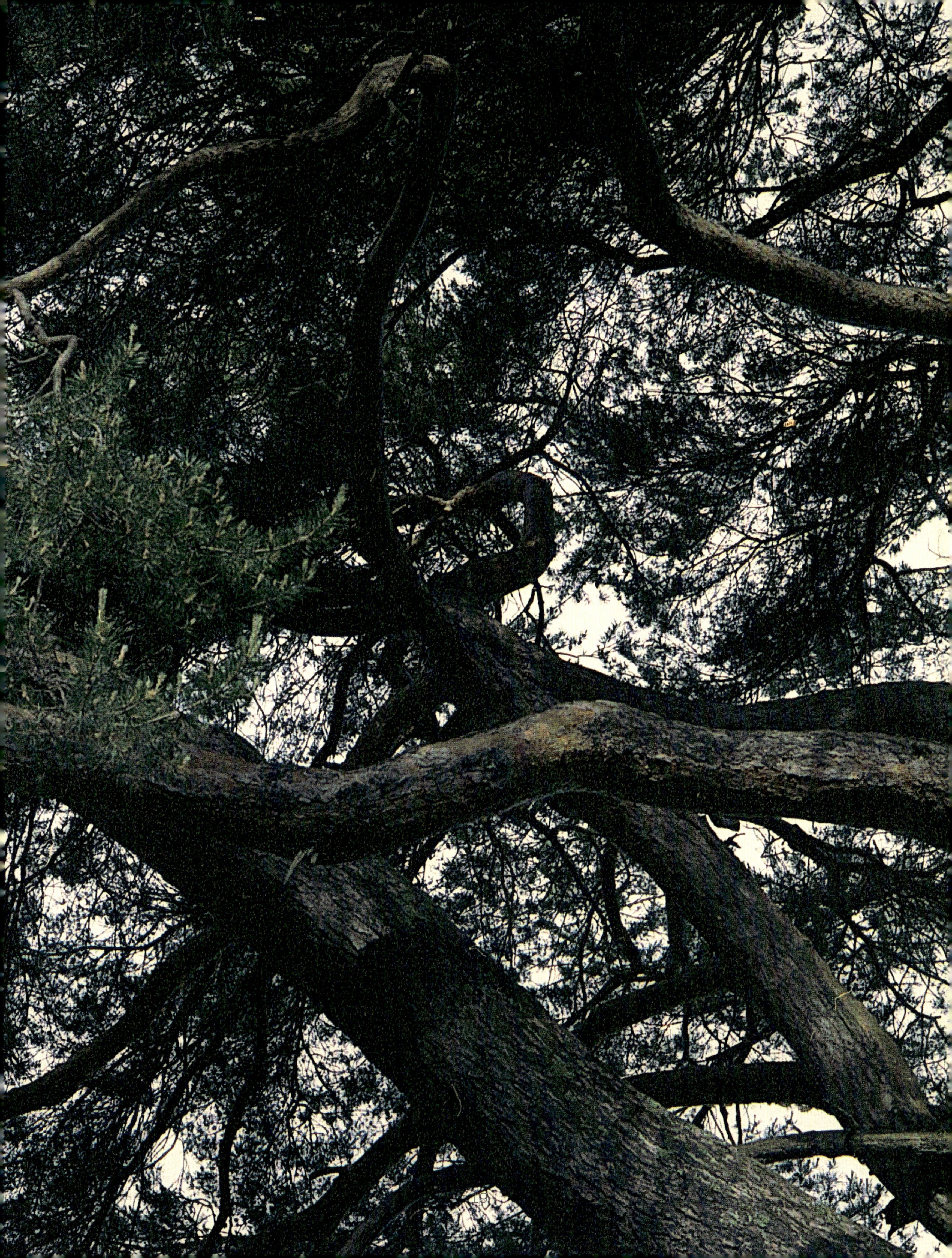

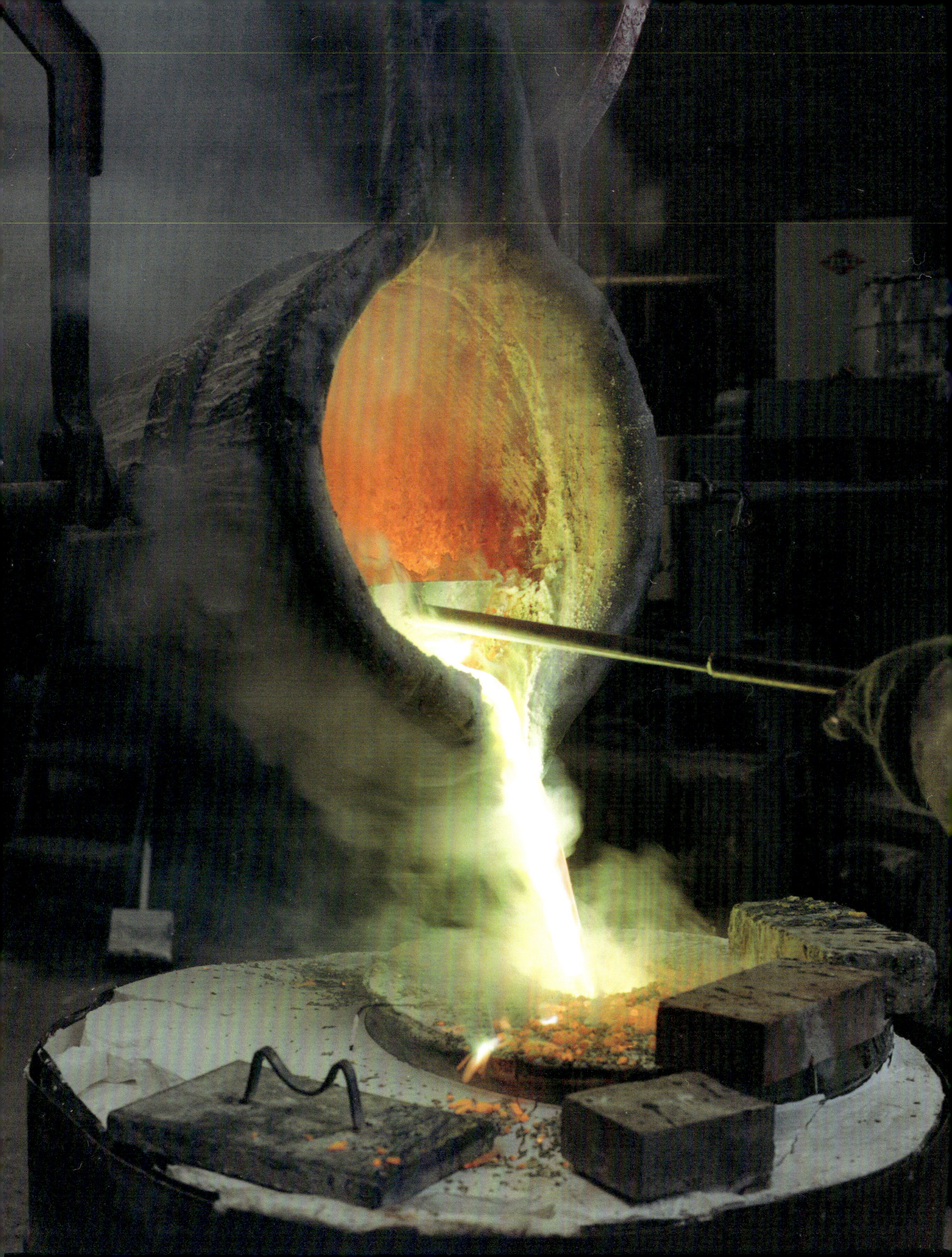

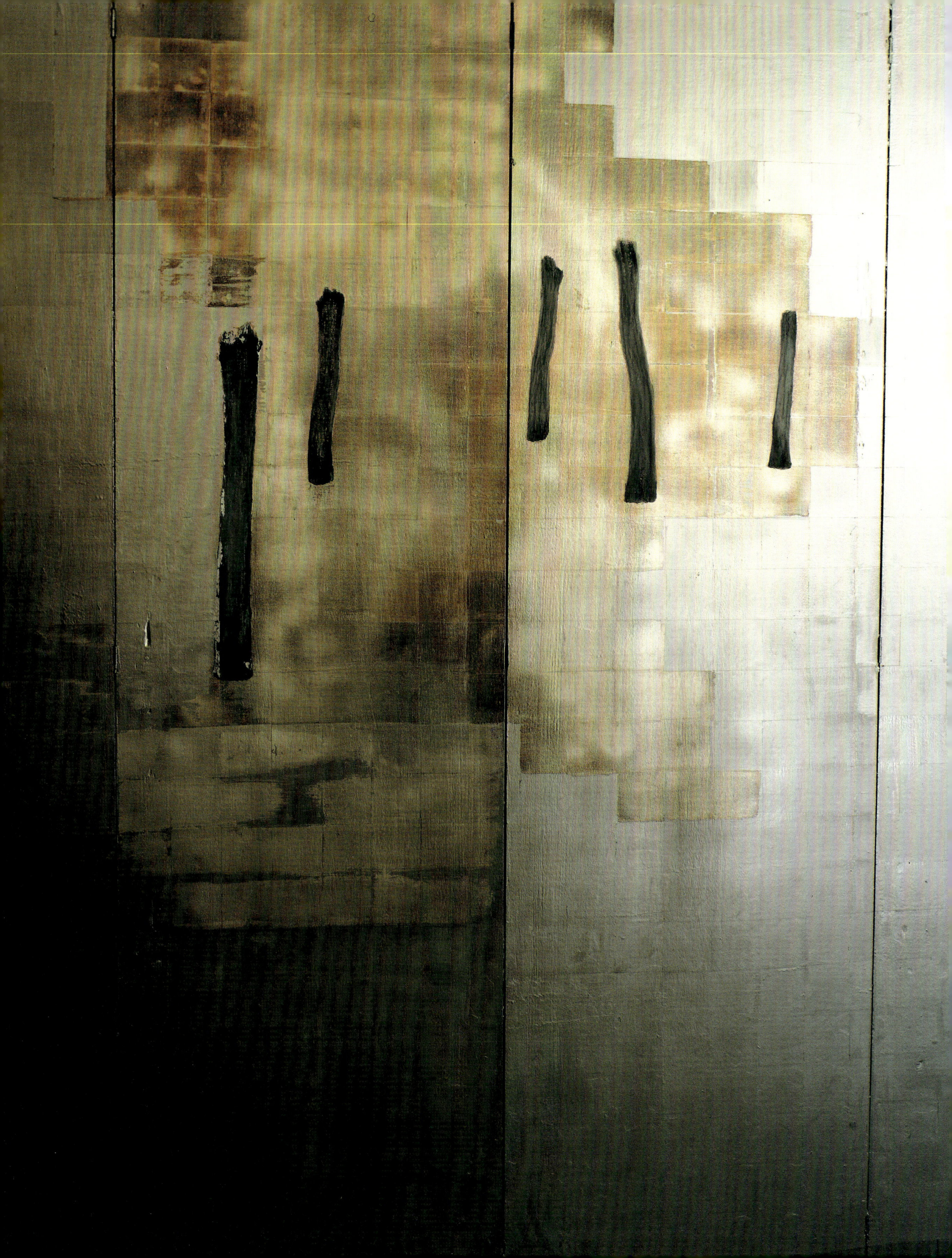

WORKS

Ame-no-kaku

2022

Bronze
Edition of eight plus two artist's proofs
81 1/8 × 76 × 16 7/8 inches (206 × 193 × 43 cm)
Fonderie de Coubertin, Saint-Rémy-lès-Chevreuse, France

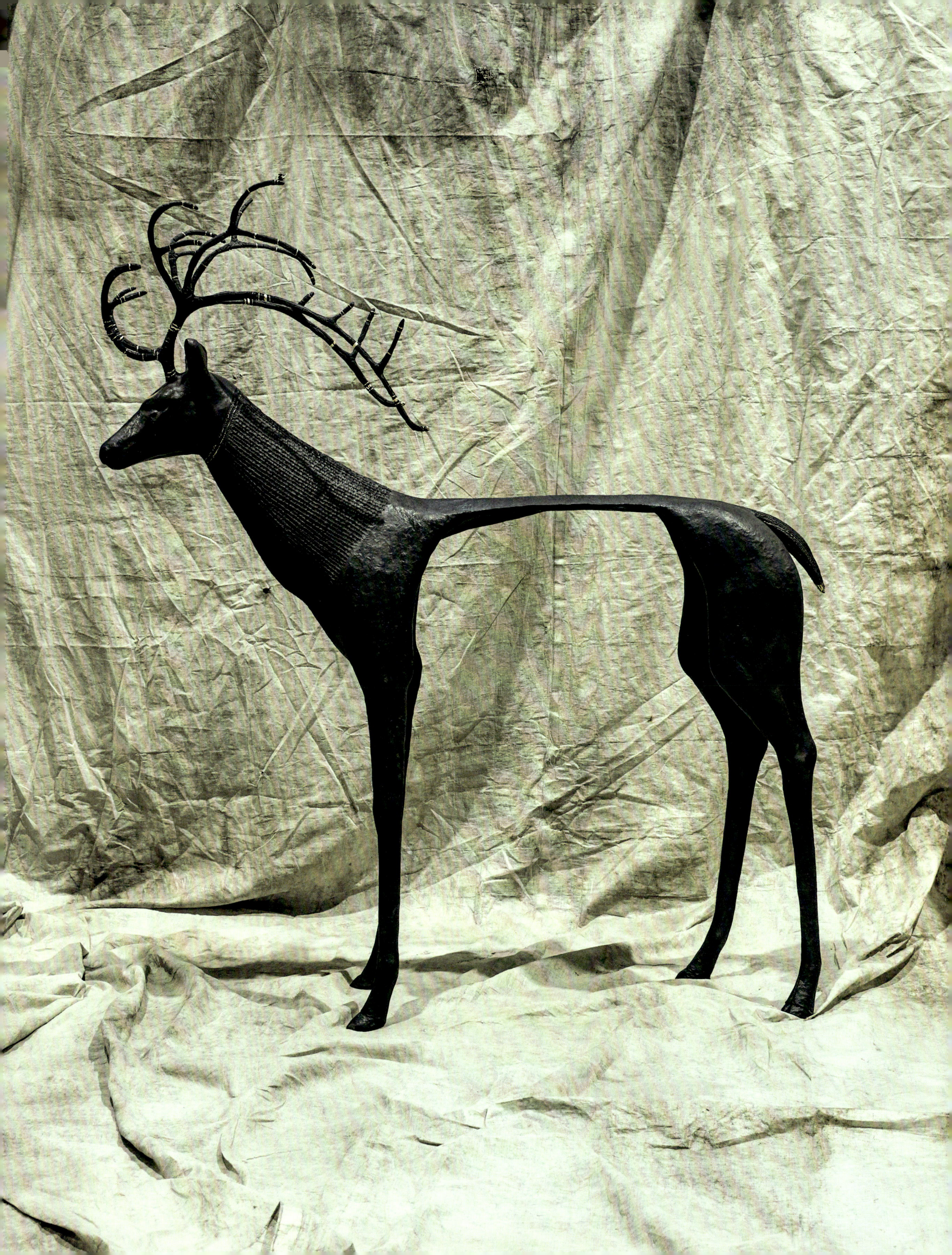

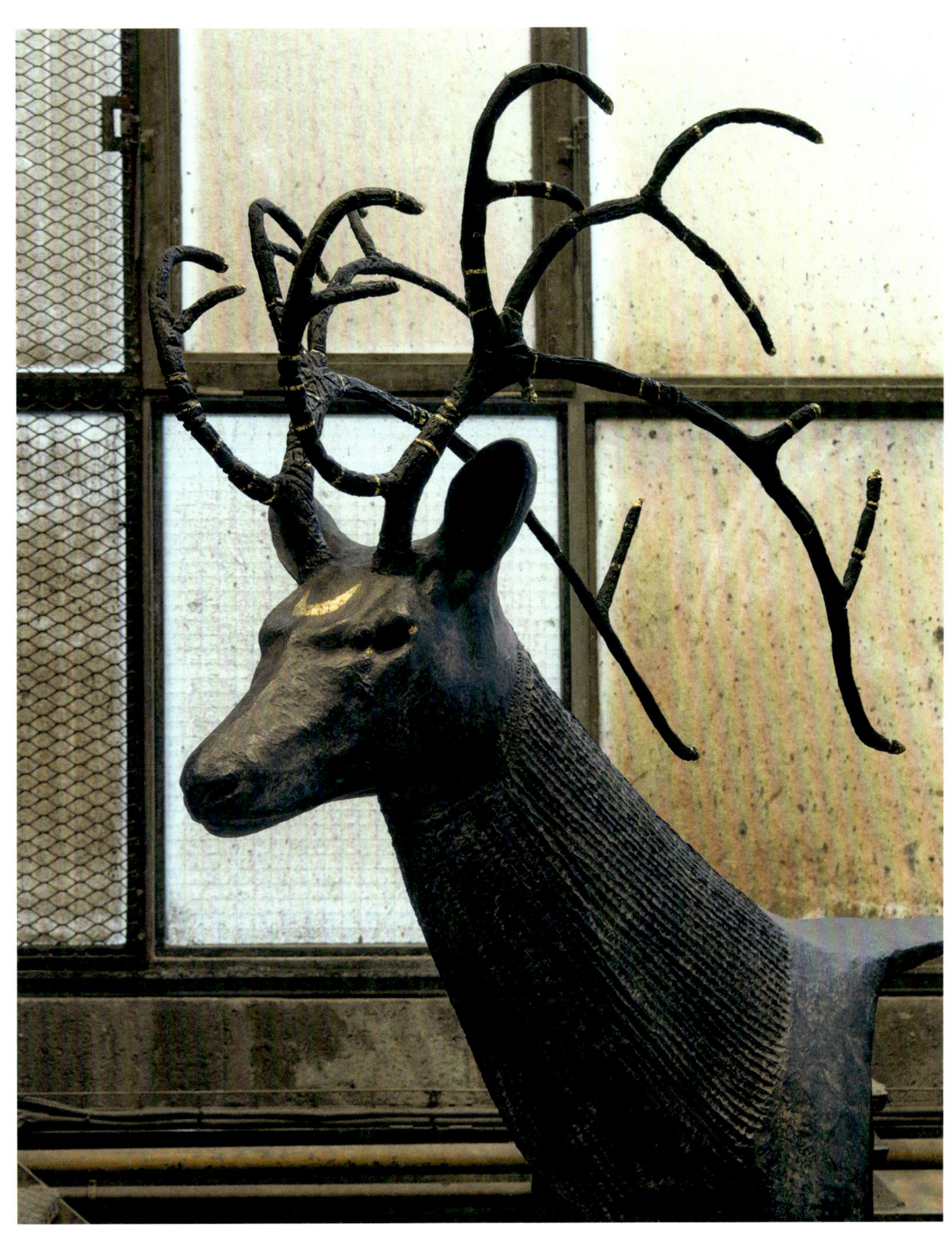

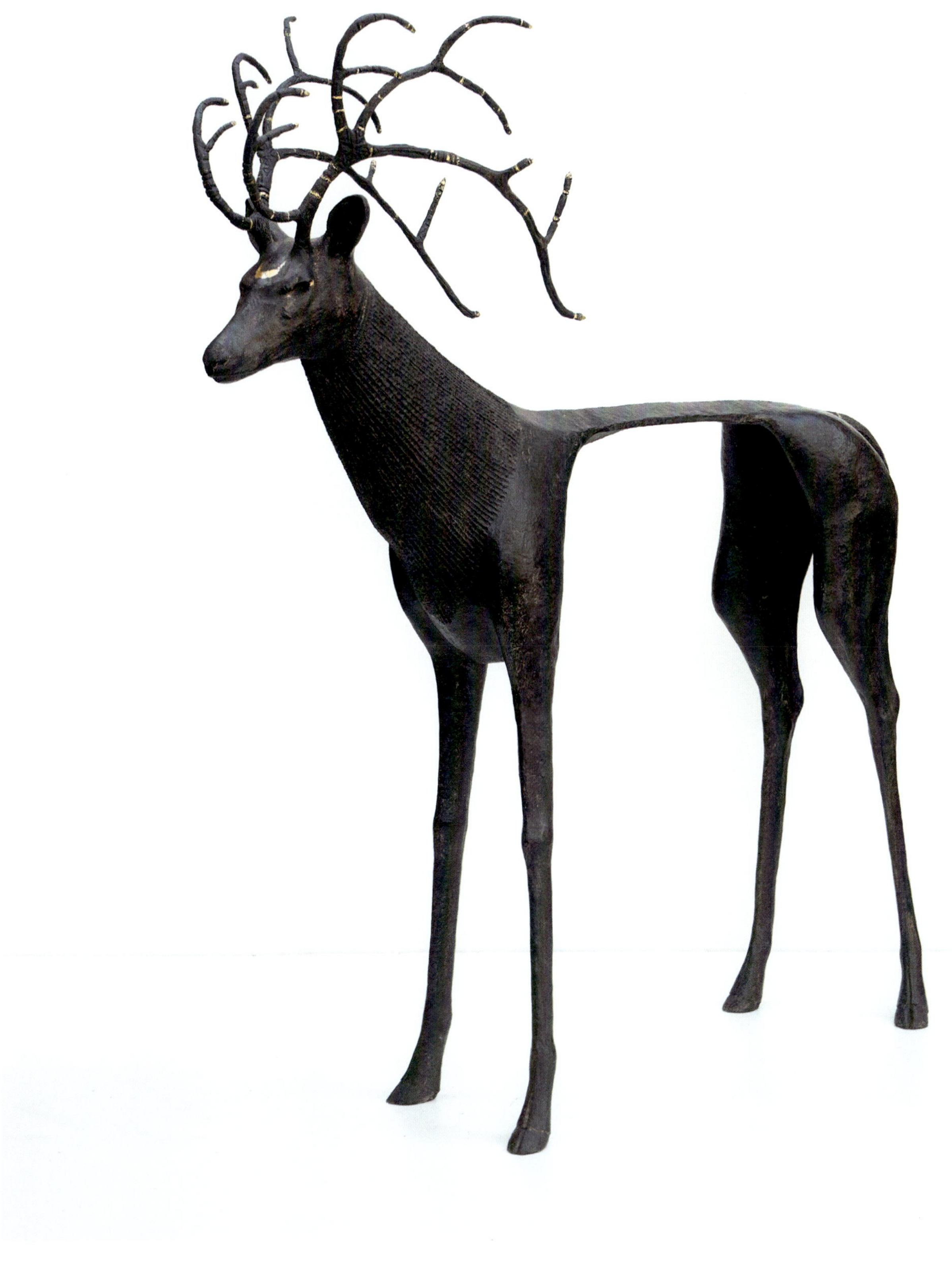

Olive Tree with Owl

2024

Bronze

Edition of eight plus two artist's proofs

74 3/4 × 19 3/4 inches (190 × 50 cm)

Fonderie de Coubertin, Saint-Rémy-lès-Chevreuse, France

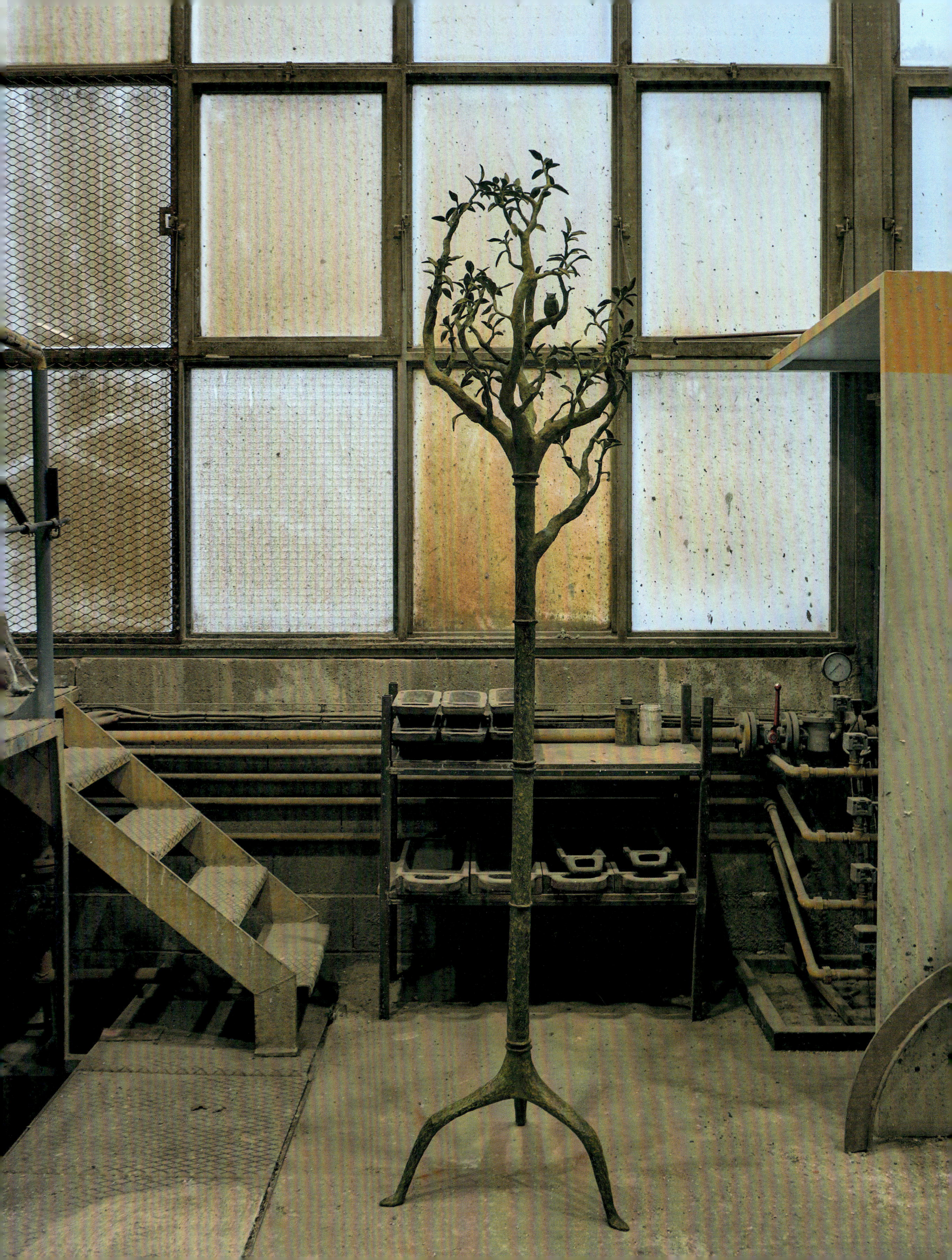

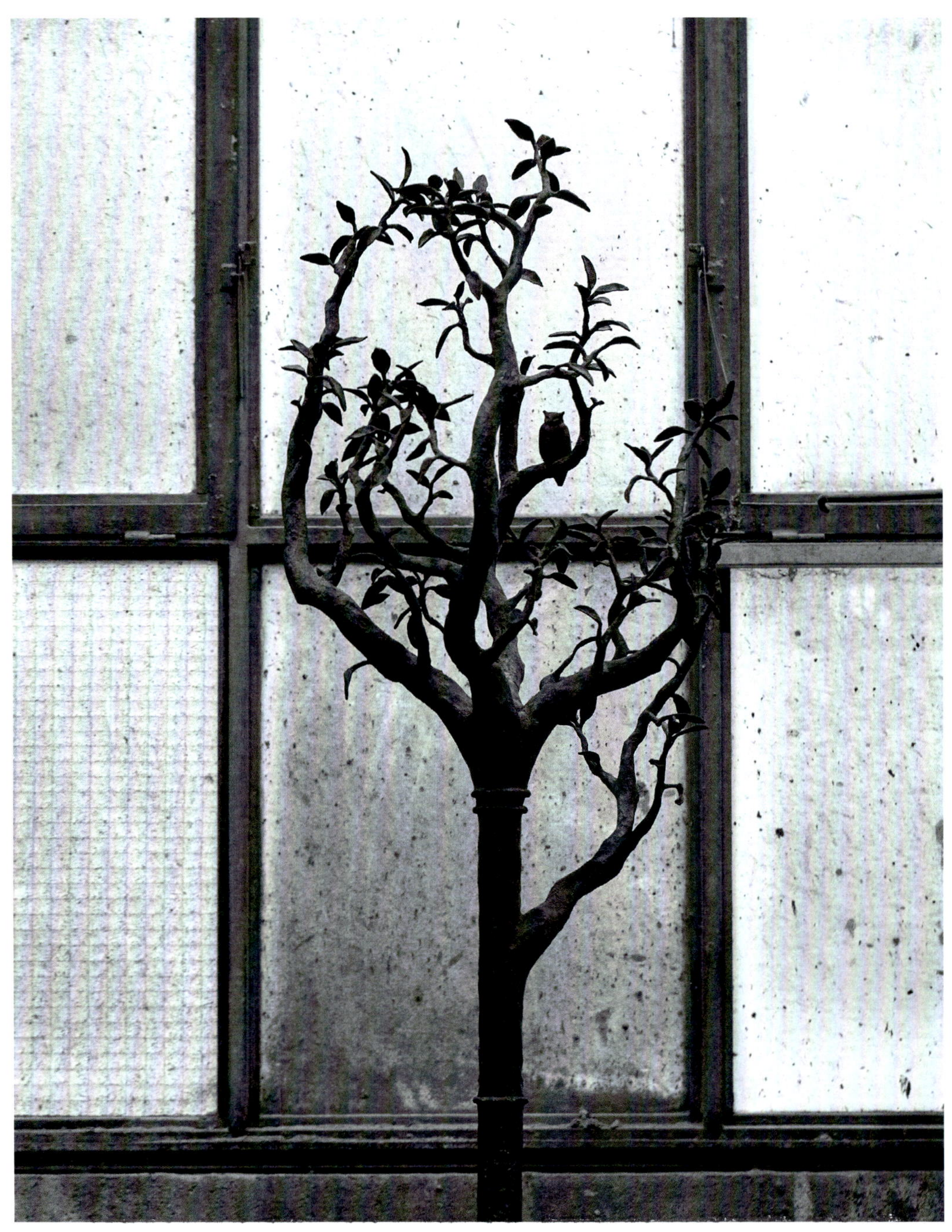

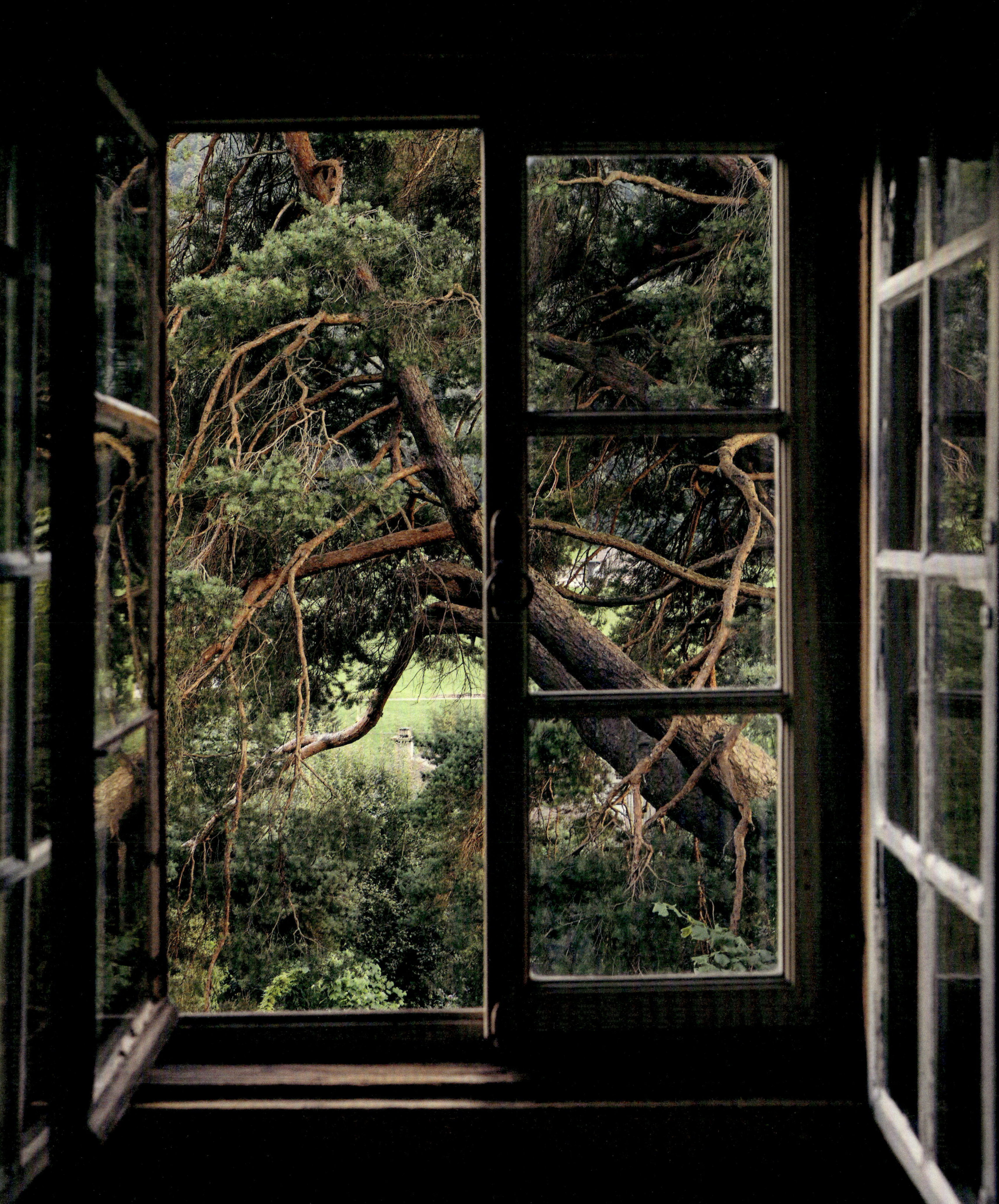

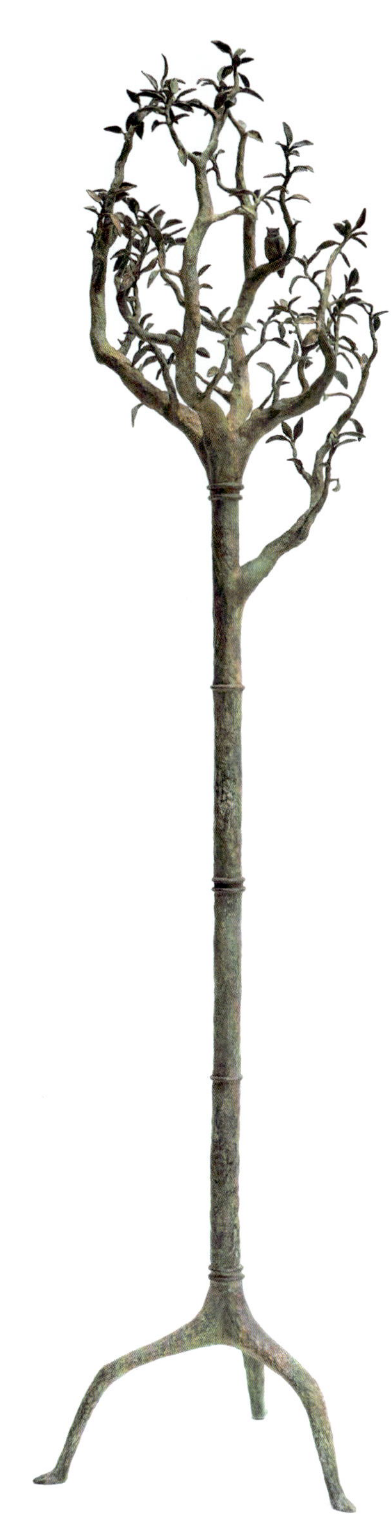

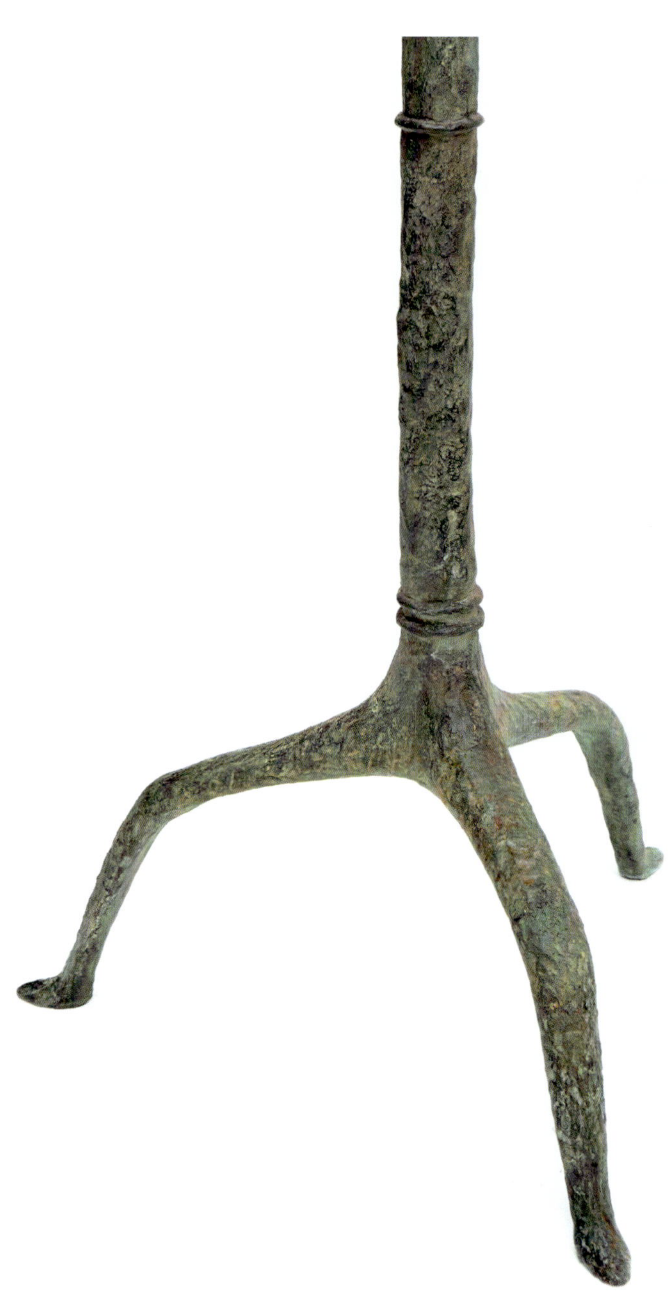

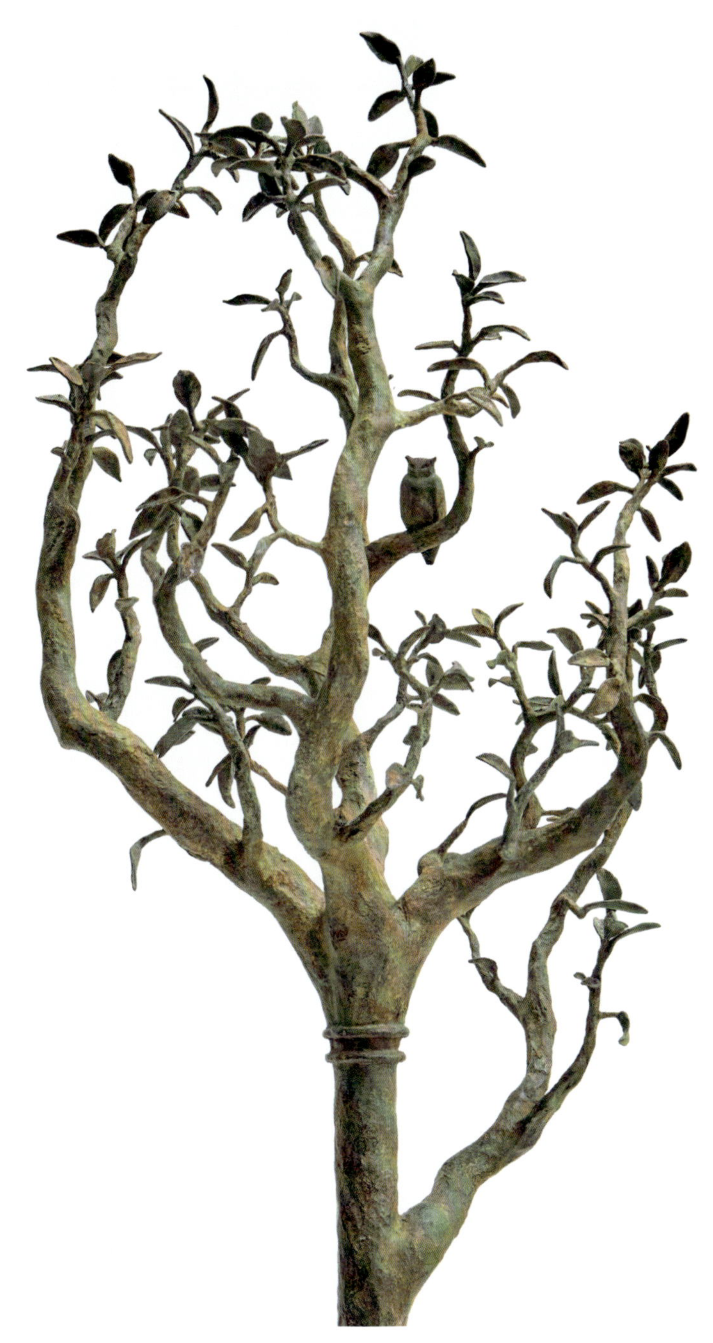

Athene Noctua

2022

Bronze

Edition of eight plus four artist's proofs

7 7/8 × 6 1/4 × 5 7/8 inches (20 × 16 × 15 cm)

Fonderie de Coubertin, Saint-Rémy-lès-Chevreuse, France

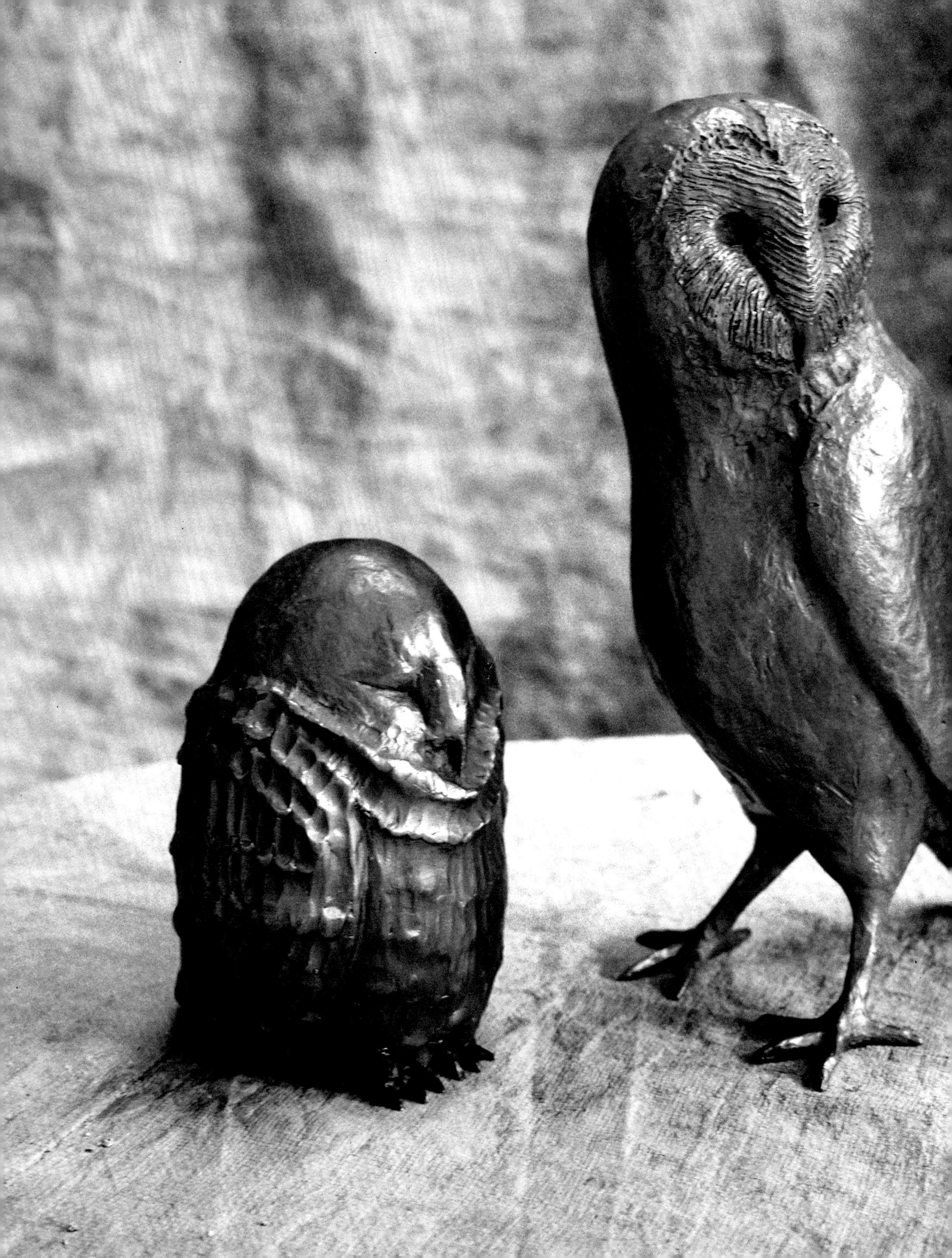

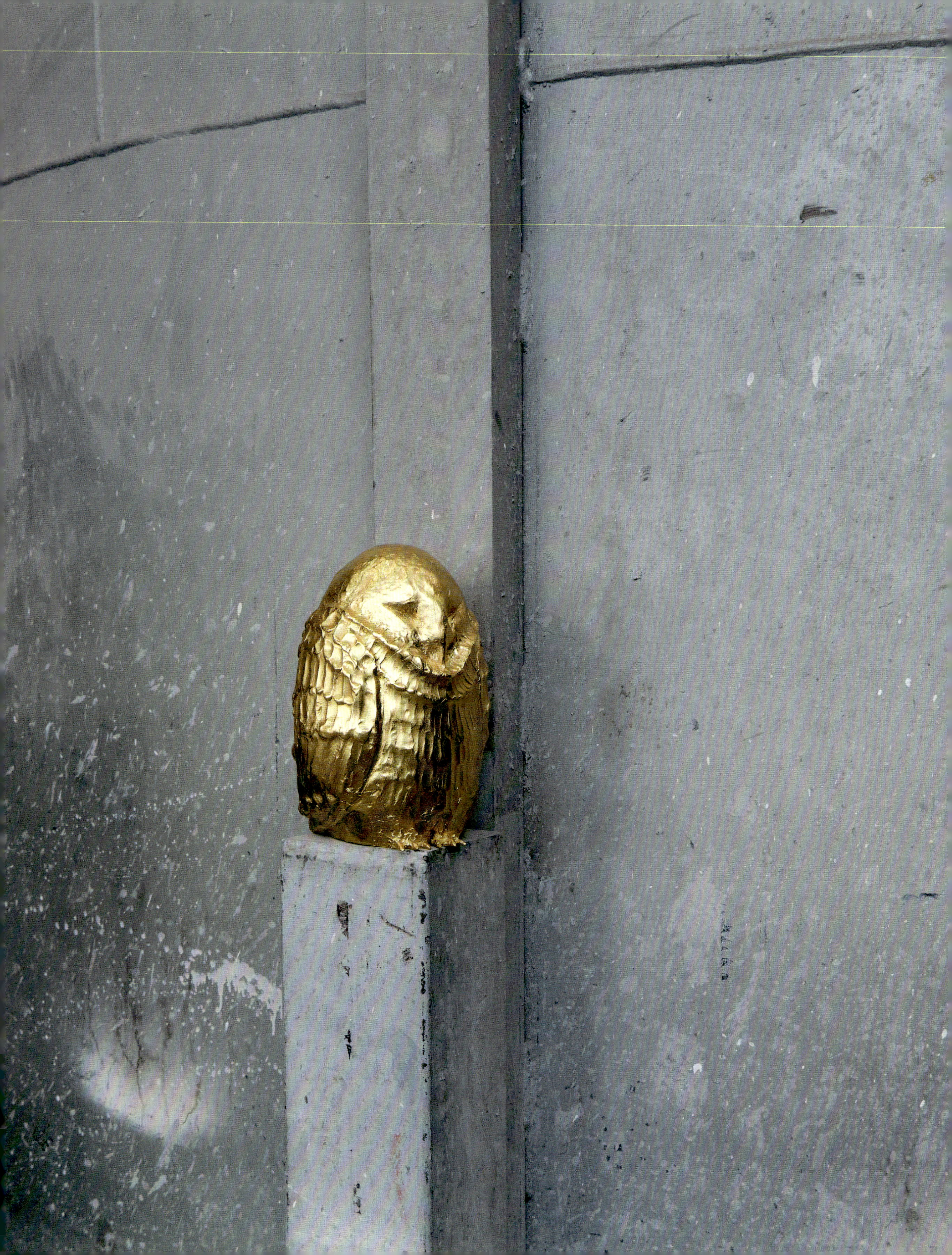

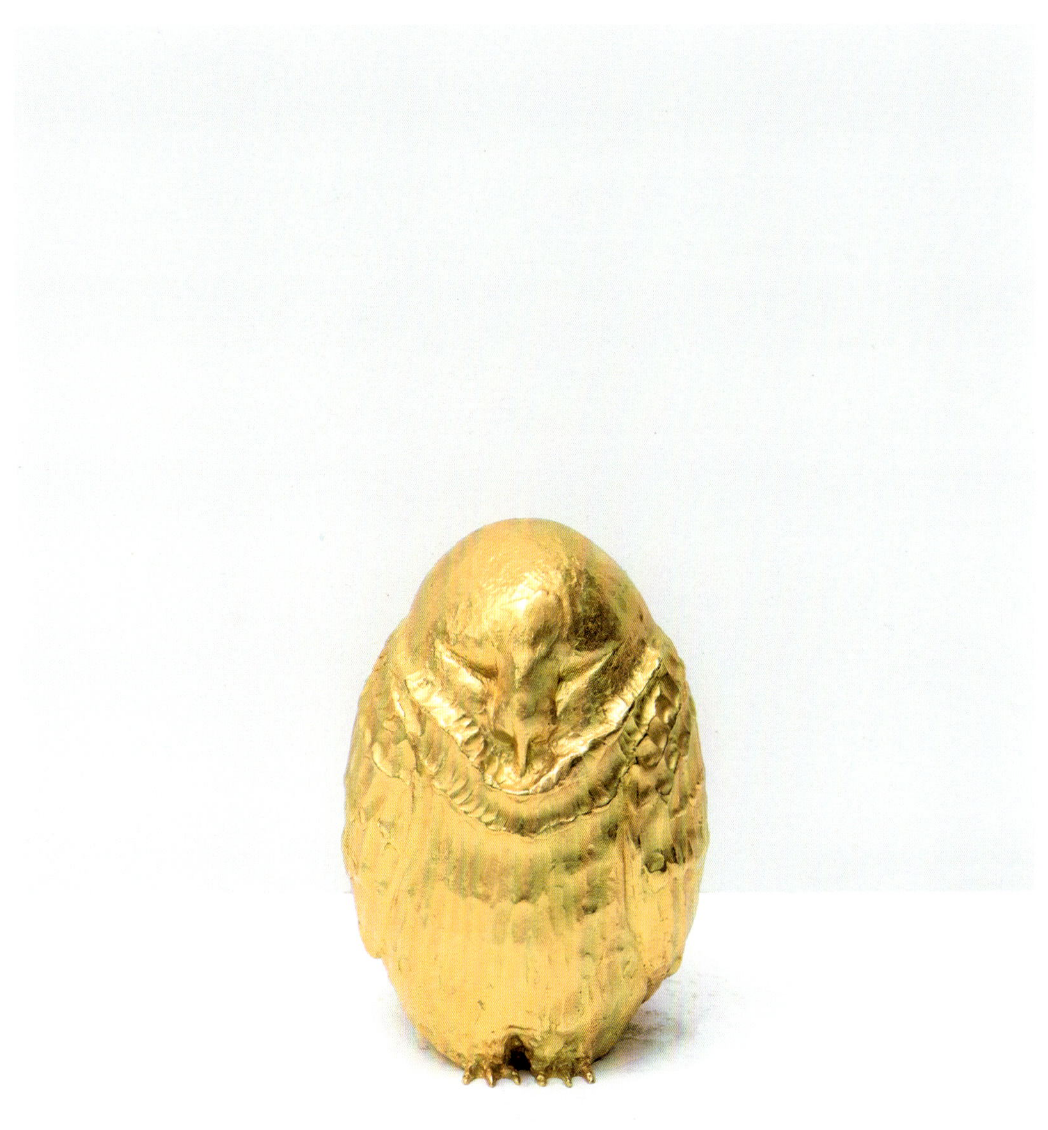

Chinook (Salmon)

2024

Bronze

Edition of eight plus two artist's proofs

11 × 31 1/2 × 4 3/4 inches (28 × 80 × 12 cm)

Fonderie de Coubertin, Saint-Rémy-lès-Chevreuse, France

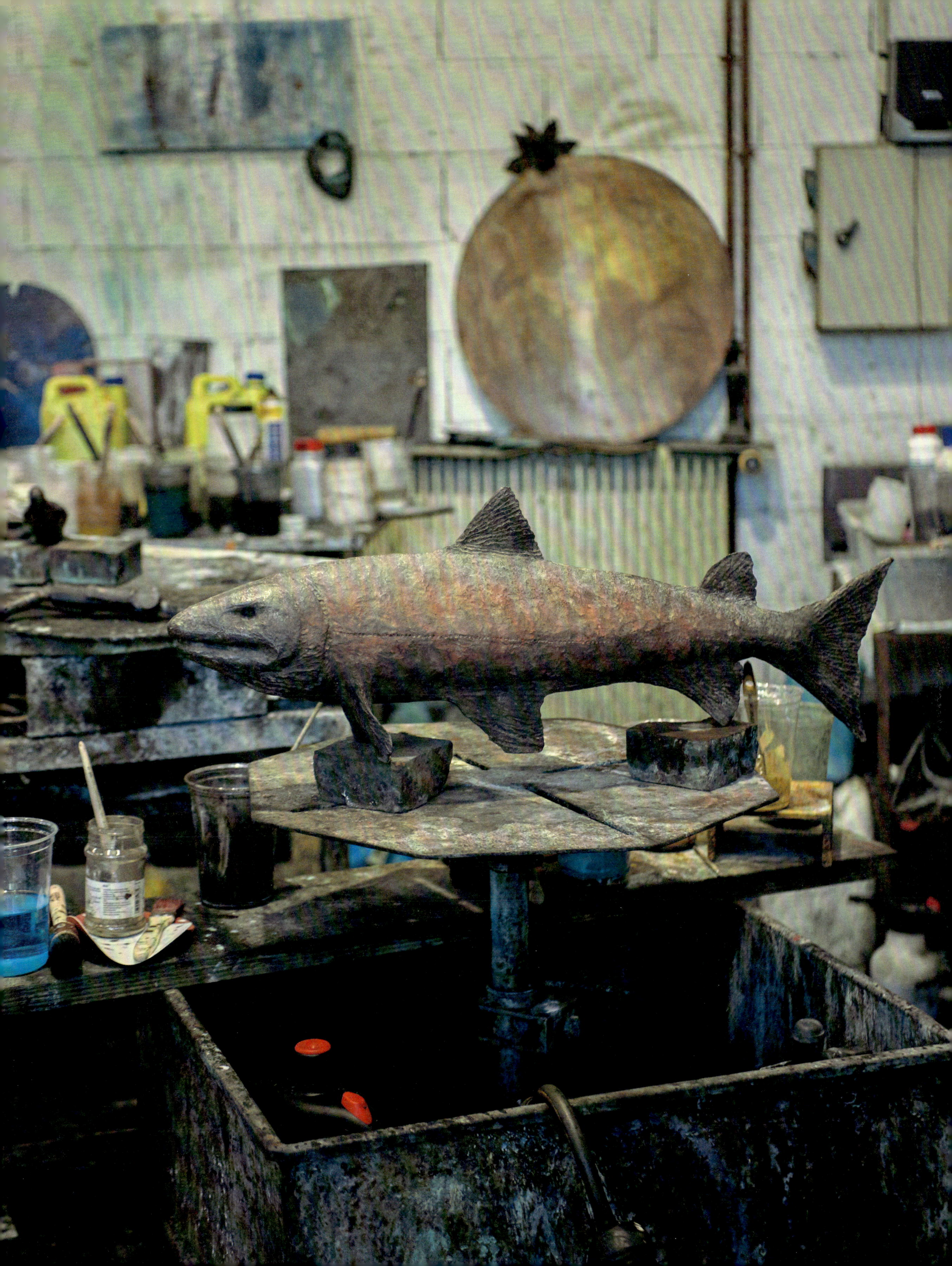

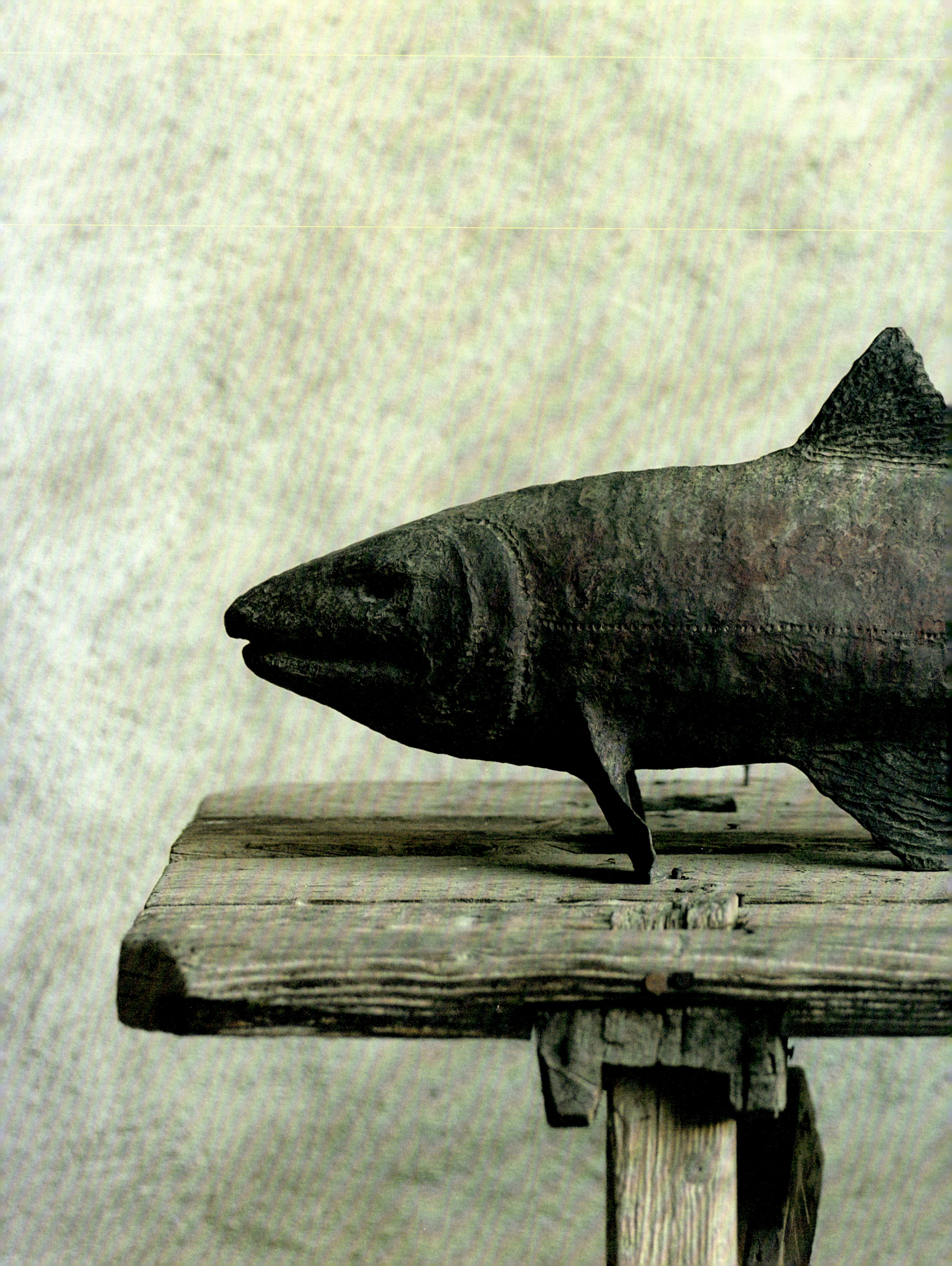

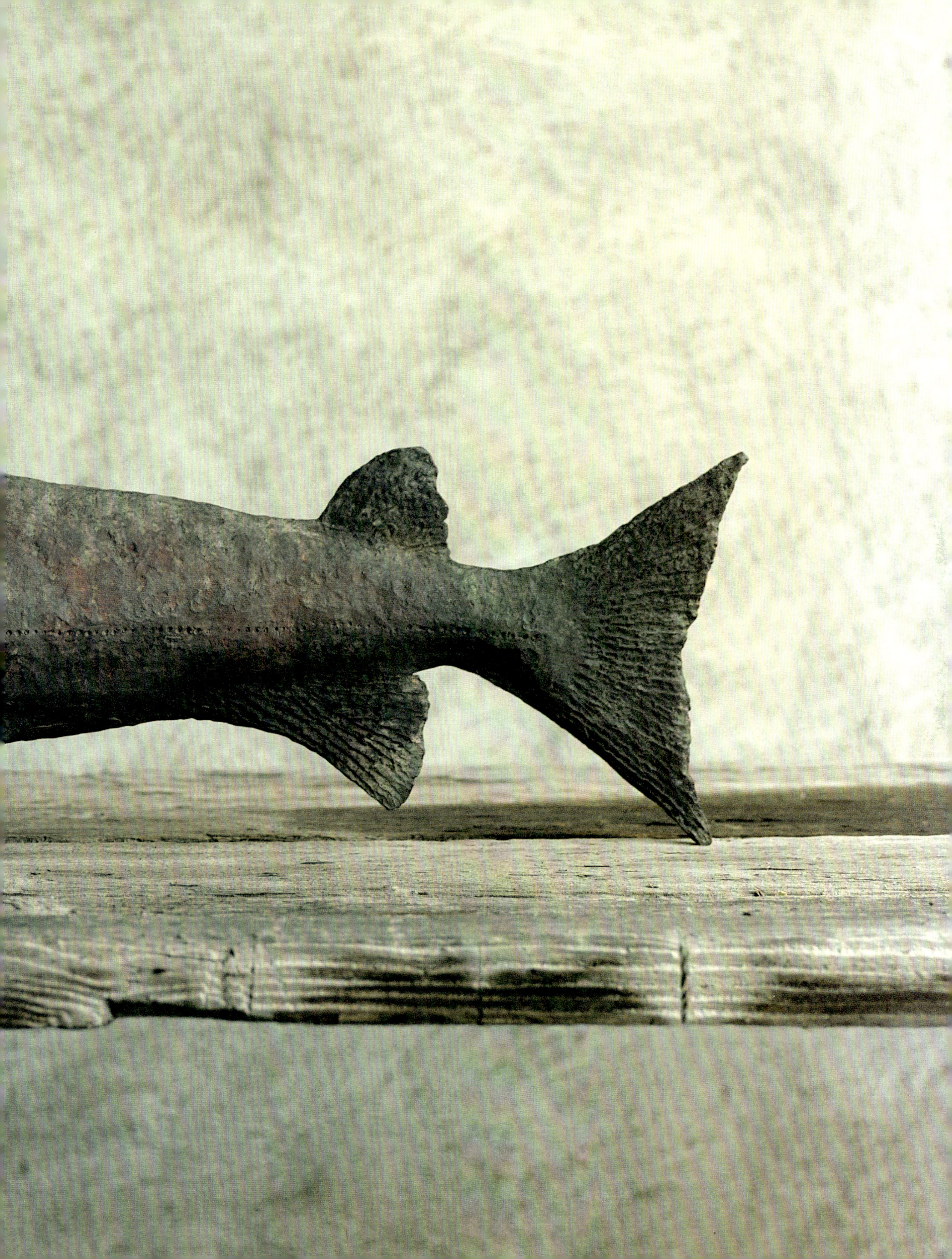

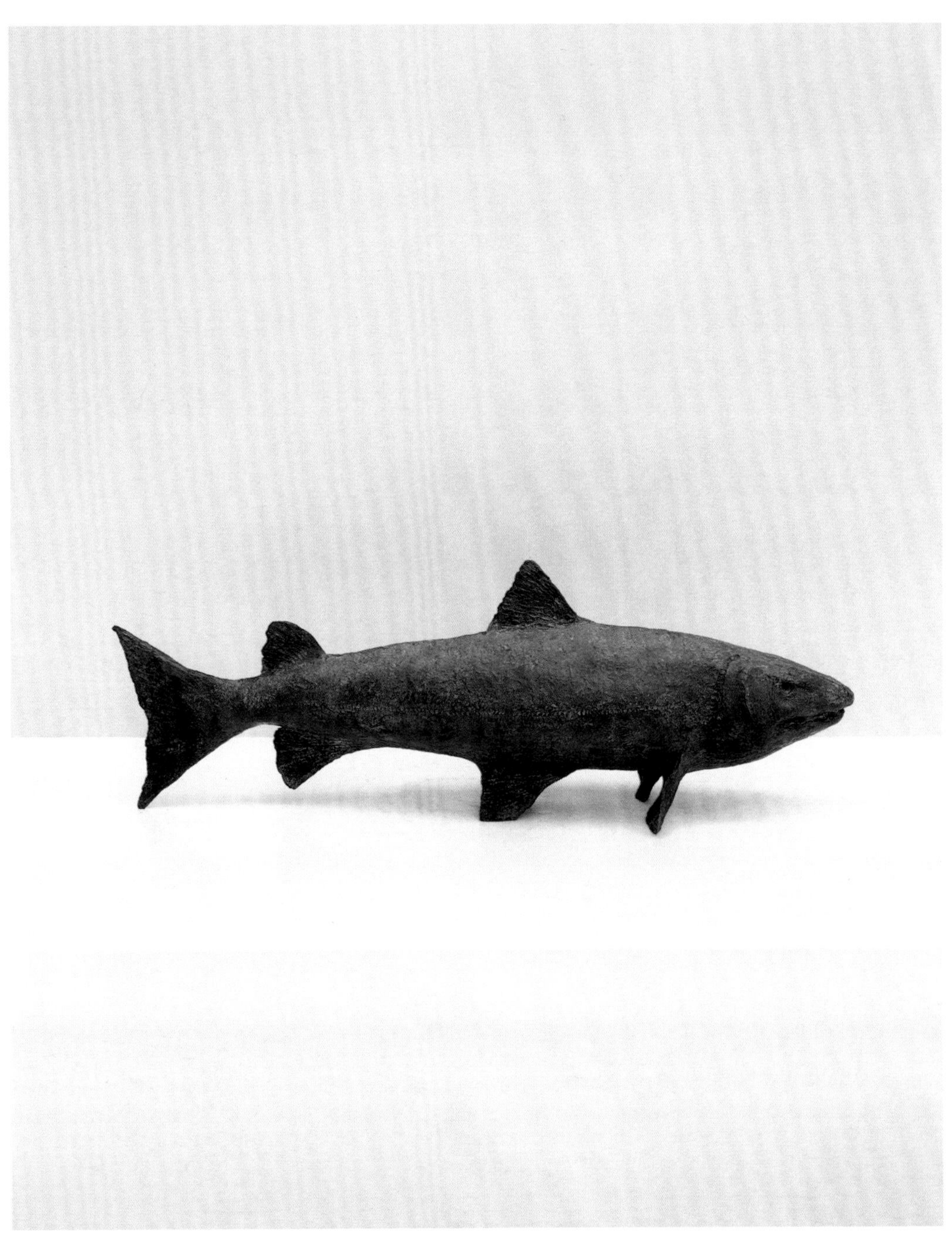

Daal

2022

Bronze
Edition of eight plus two artist's proofs
59 7/8 × 59 7/8 × 14 1/8 inches (152 × 152 × 36 cm)
Fonderie de Coubertin, Saint-Rémy-lès-Chevreuse, France

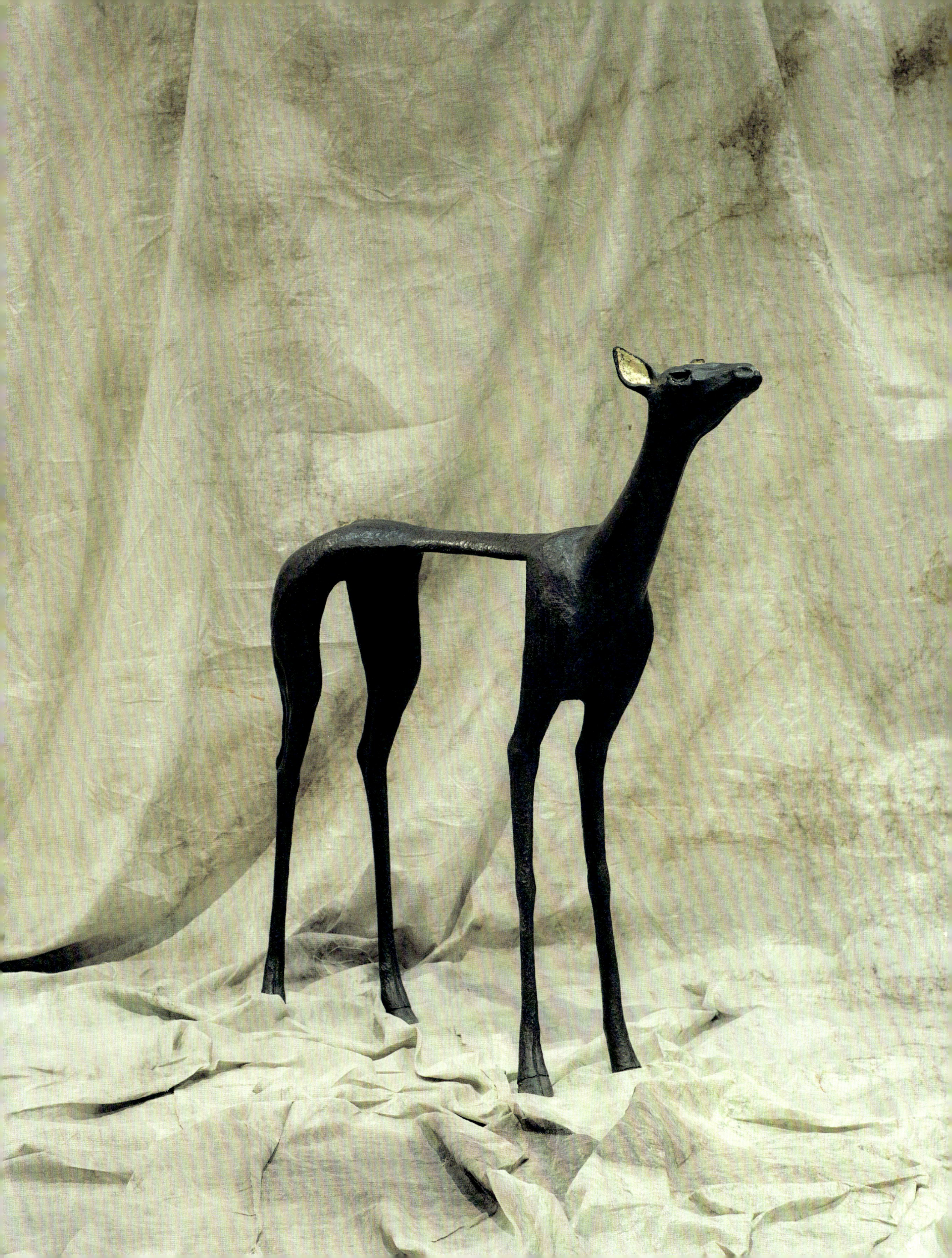

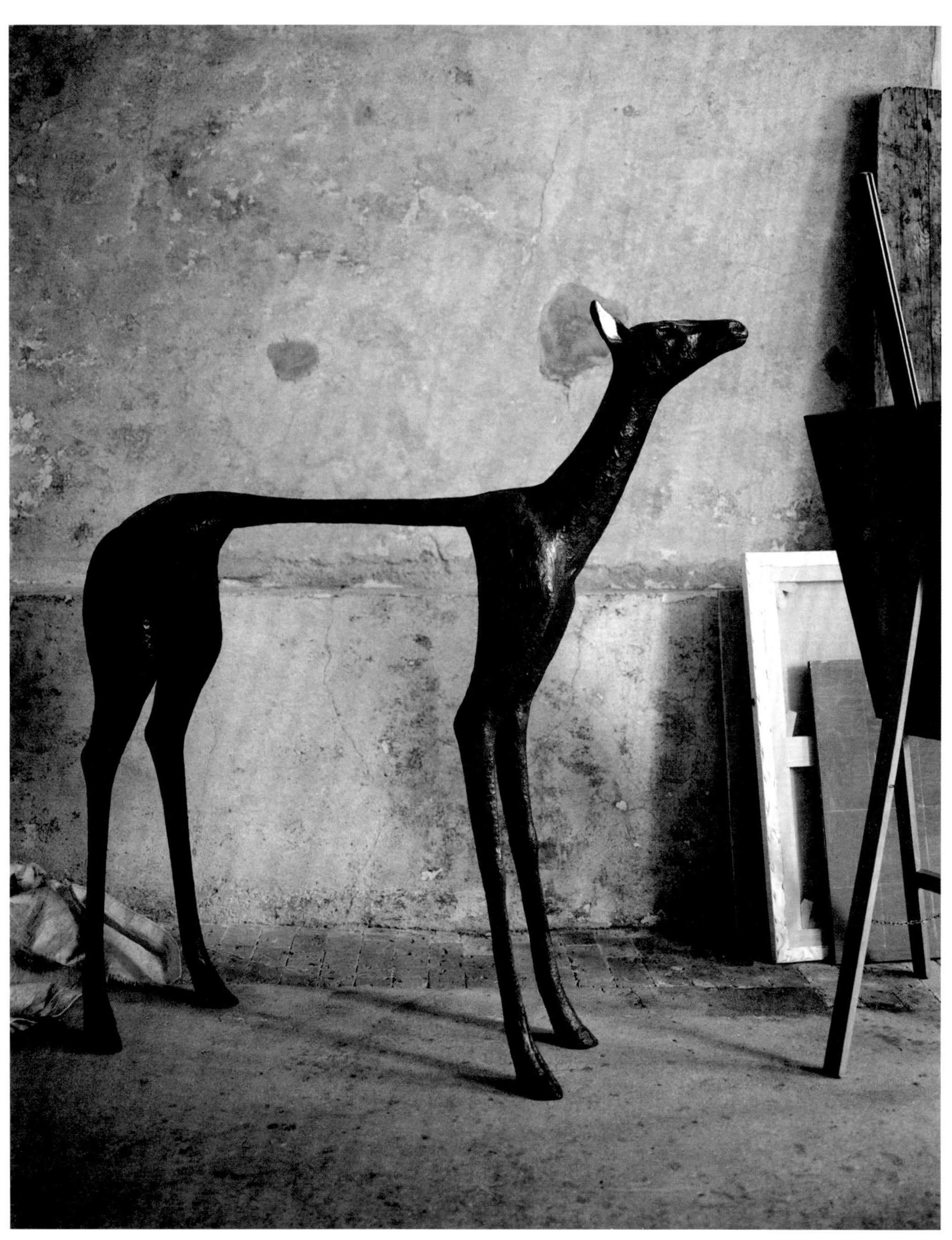

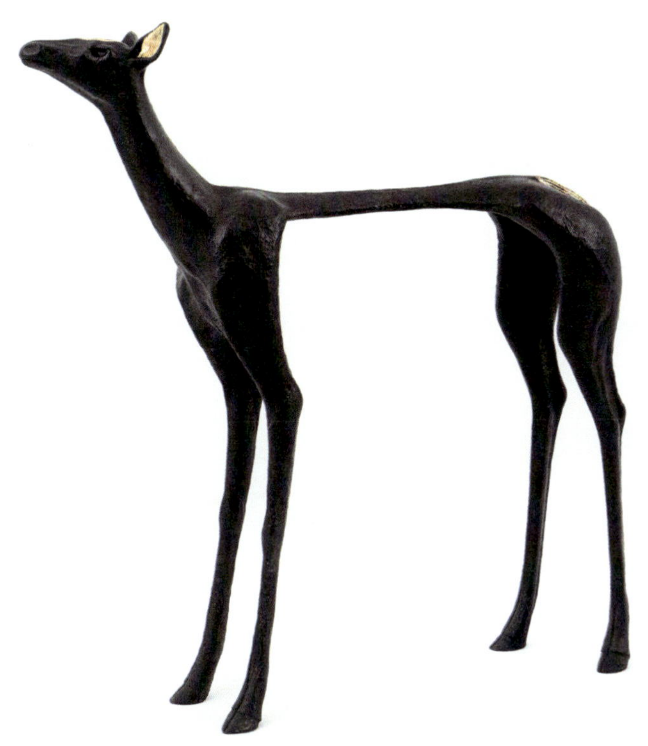

Owl in Moonlight

2024

Bronze

Edition of eight plus two artist's proofs

72 7/8 × 12 5/8 × 12 5/8 inches (185 × 32 × 32 cm) (diameter at top)

Fonderie de Coubertin, Saint-Rémy-lès-Chevreuse, France

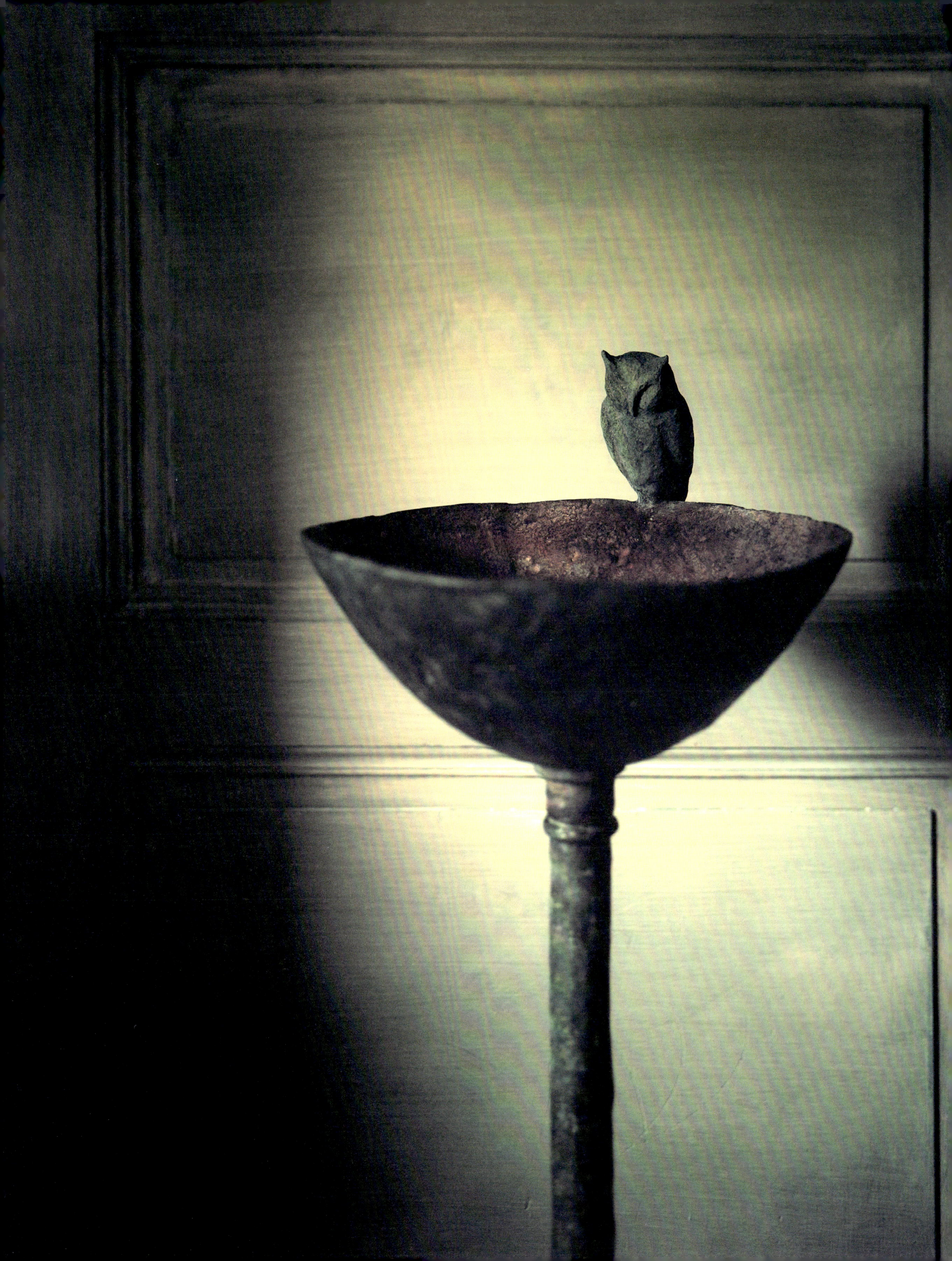

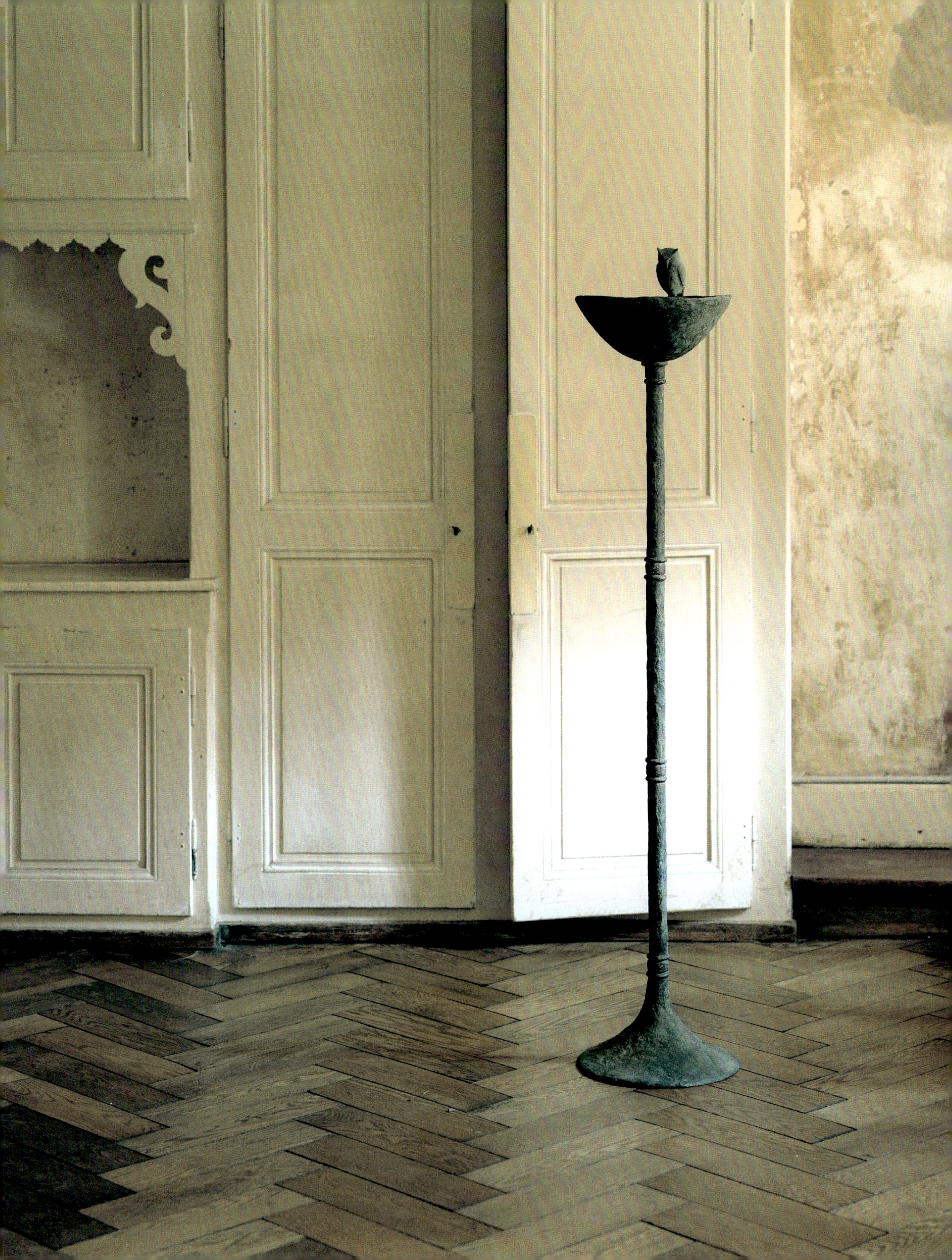

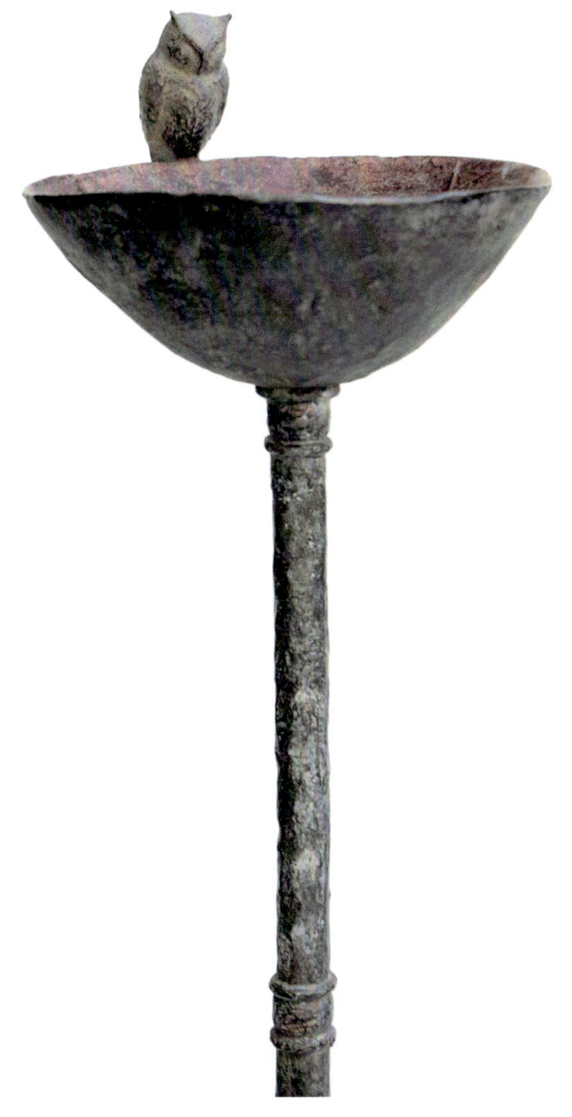

Sleeping Dove (Laying Bird)
2024

Alabaster and bronze
Edition of eight plus two artist's proofs
$7\frac{7}{8} \times 11\frac{3}{4}$ inches (20 × 30 cm)
Fonderie Patrick Laroche, Paris

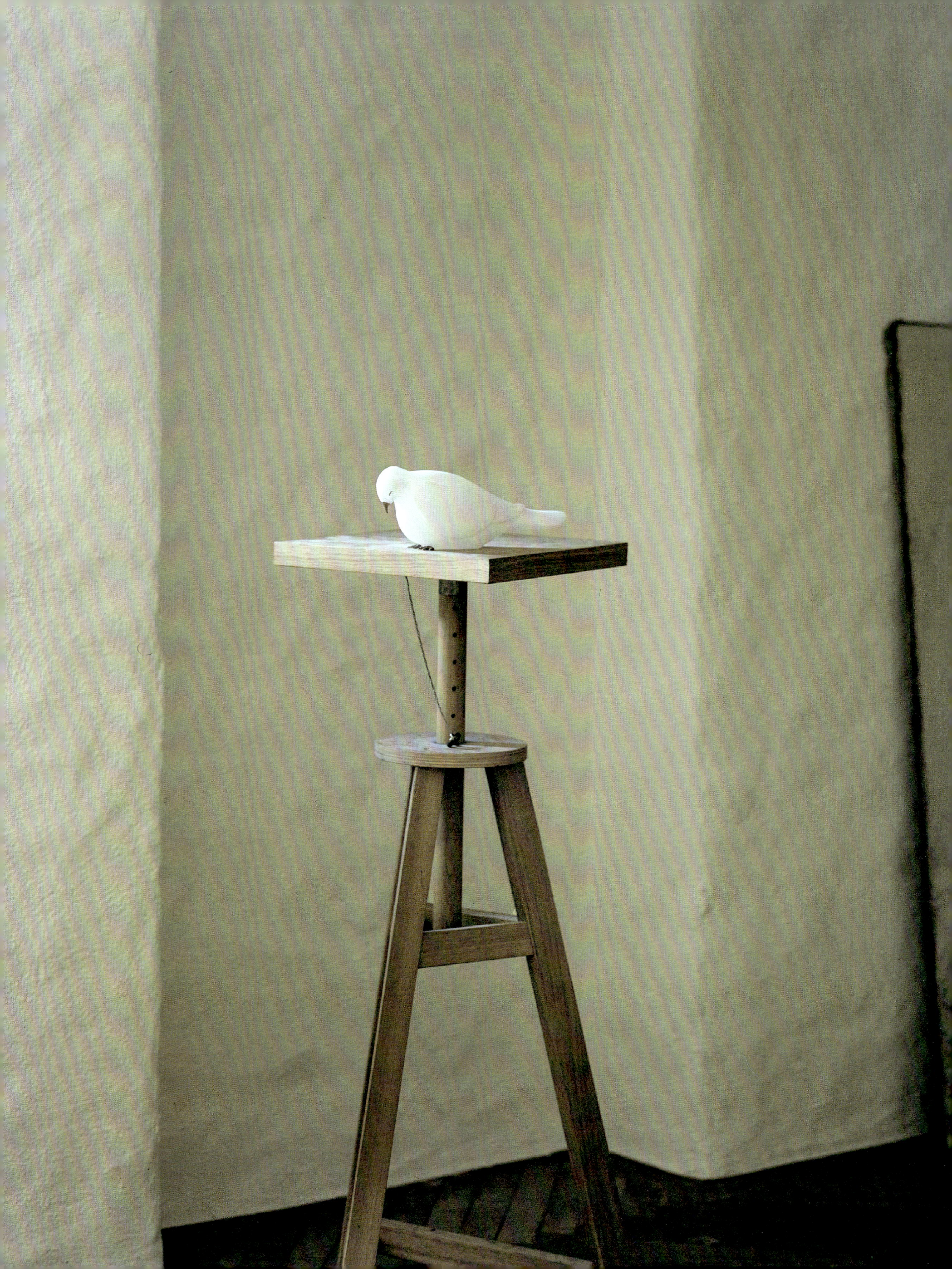

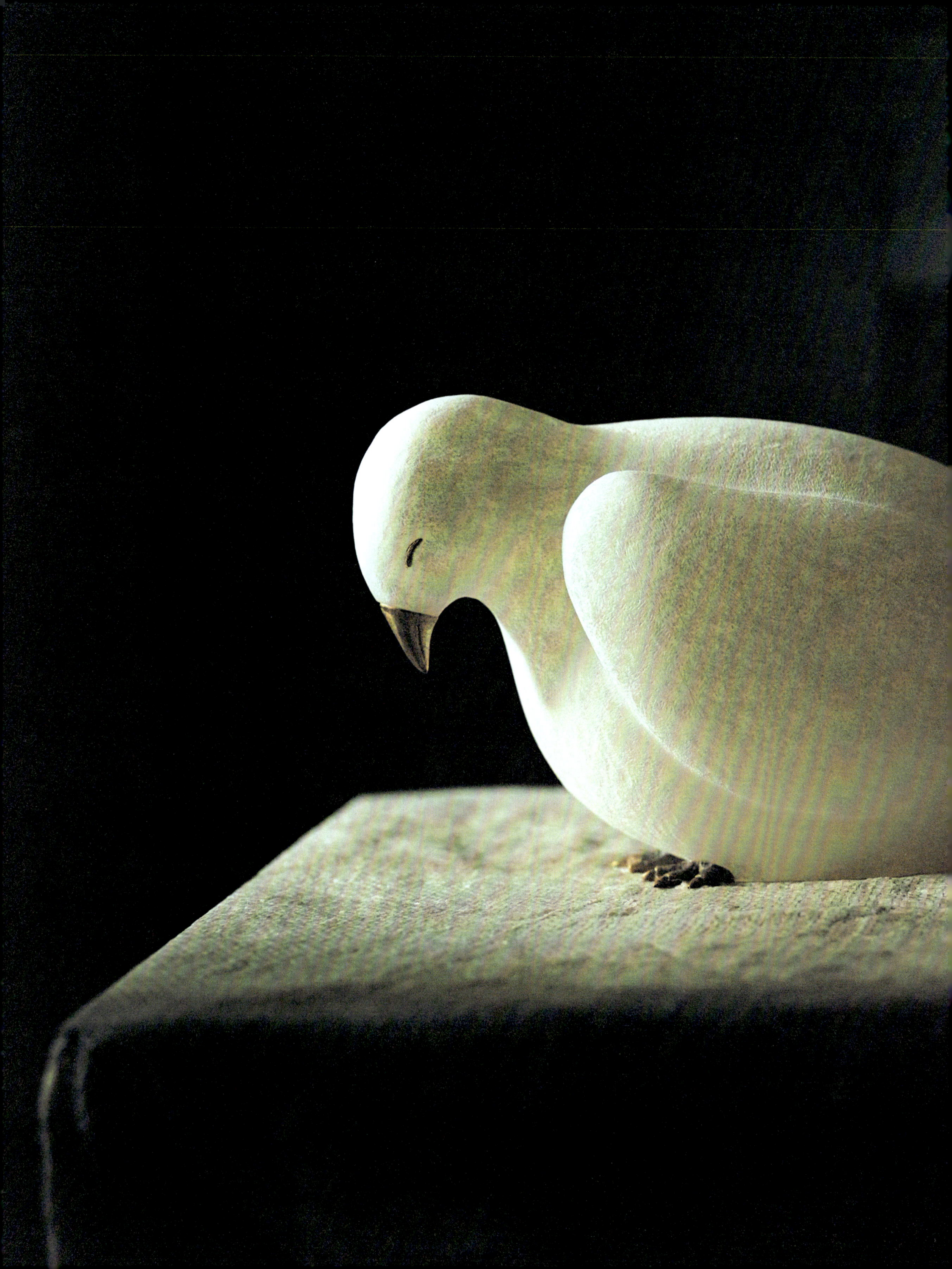

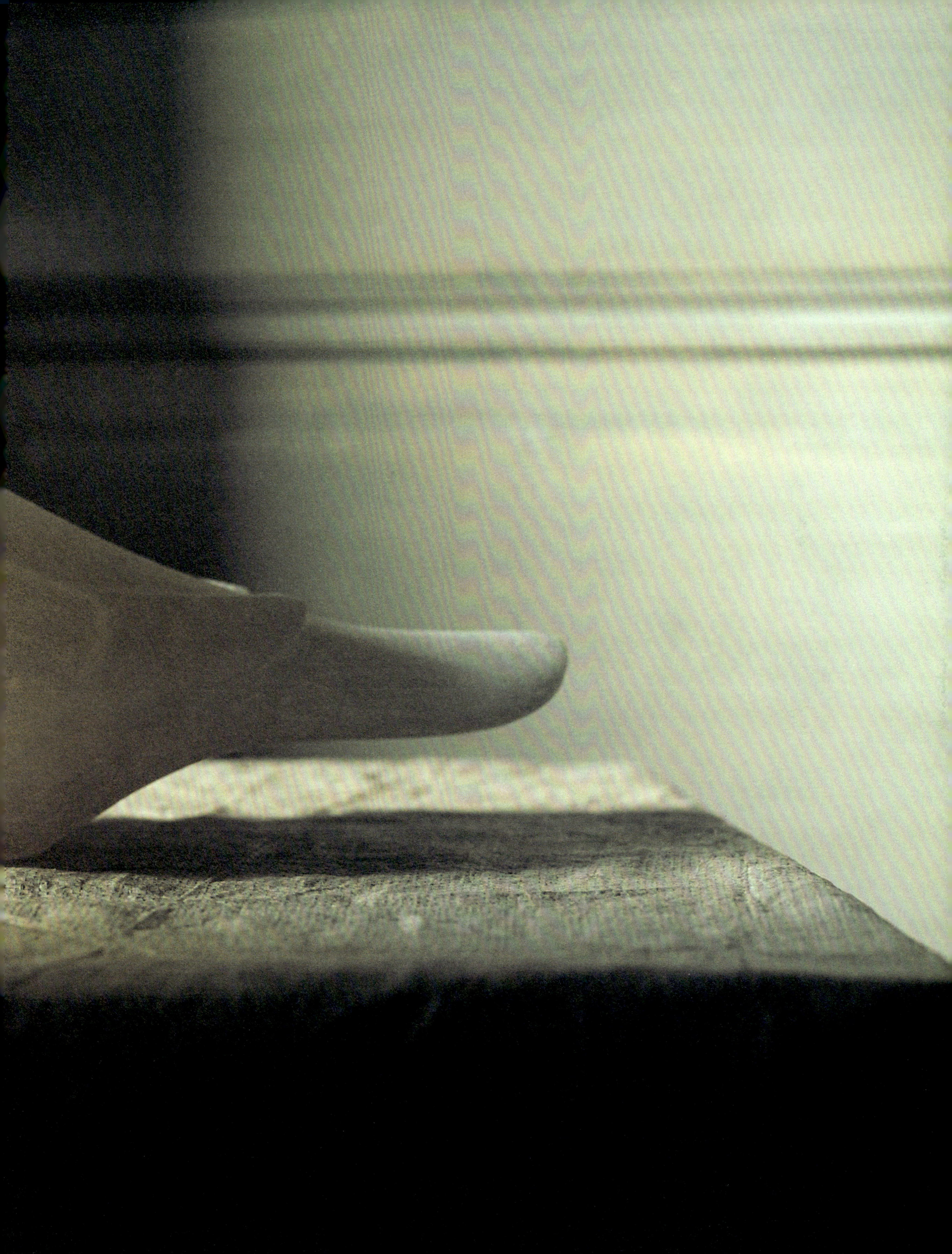

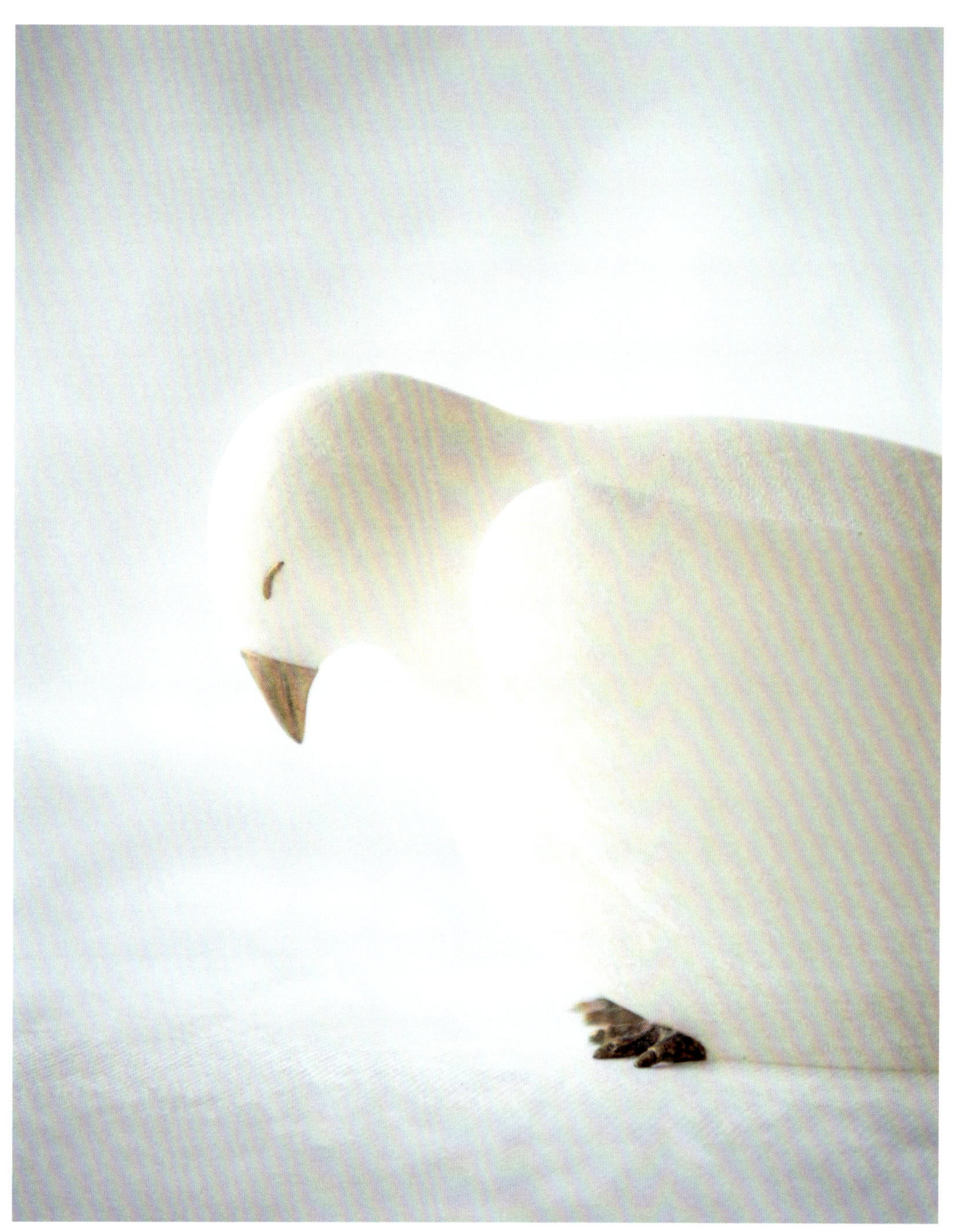

Nanuk

2024

Bronze
Edition of three plus one artist's proof
85 3/8 × 30 1/2 × 24 3/4 inches (217 × 77.5 × 63 cm)
Fonderie de Coubertin, Saint-Rémy-lès-Chevreuse, France

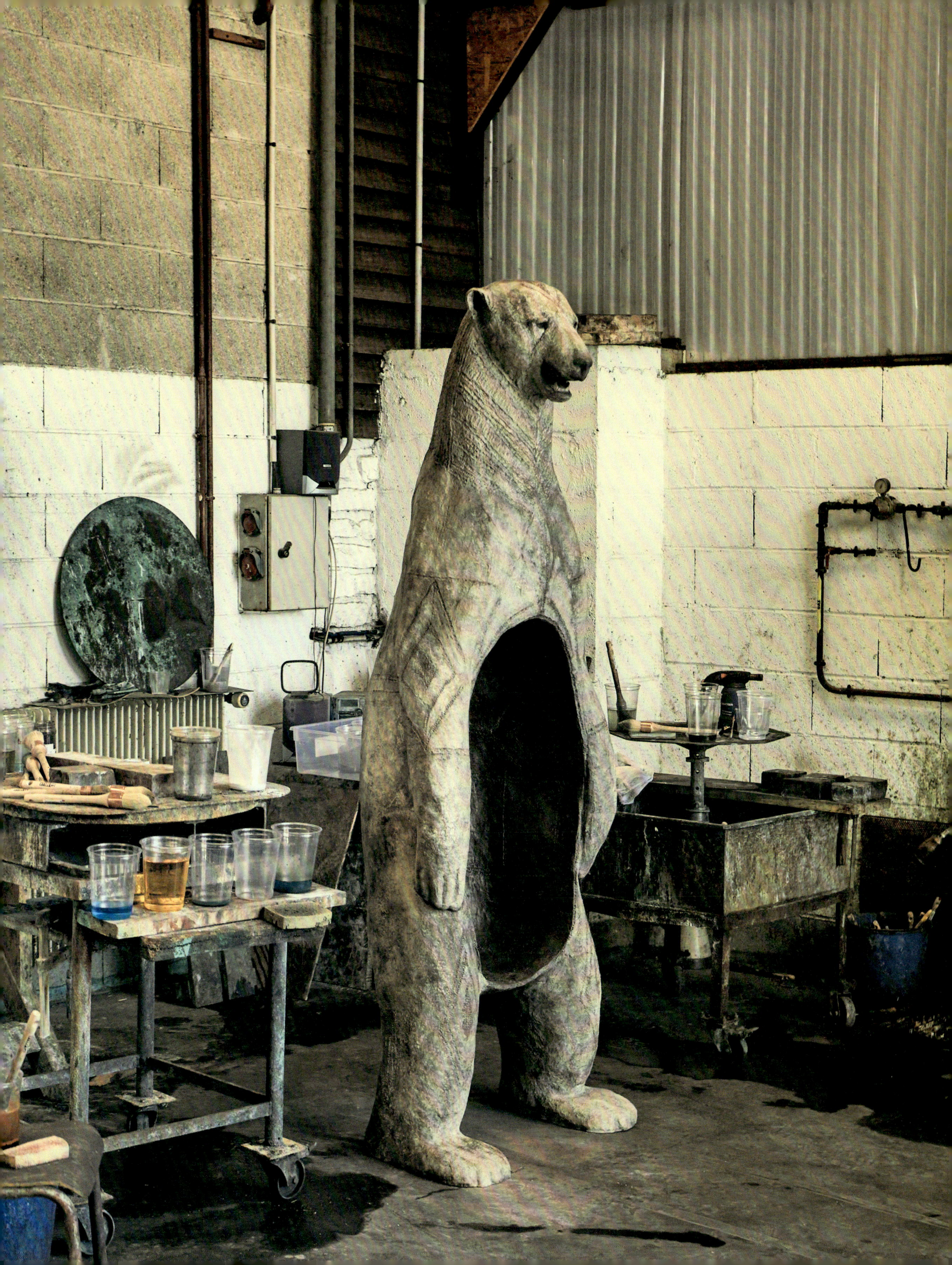

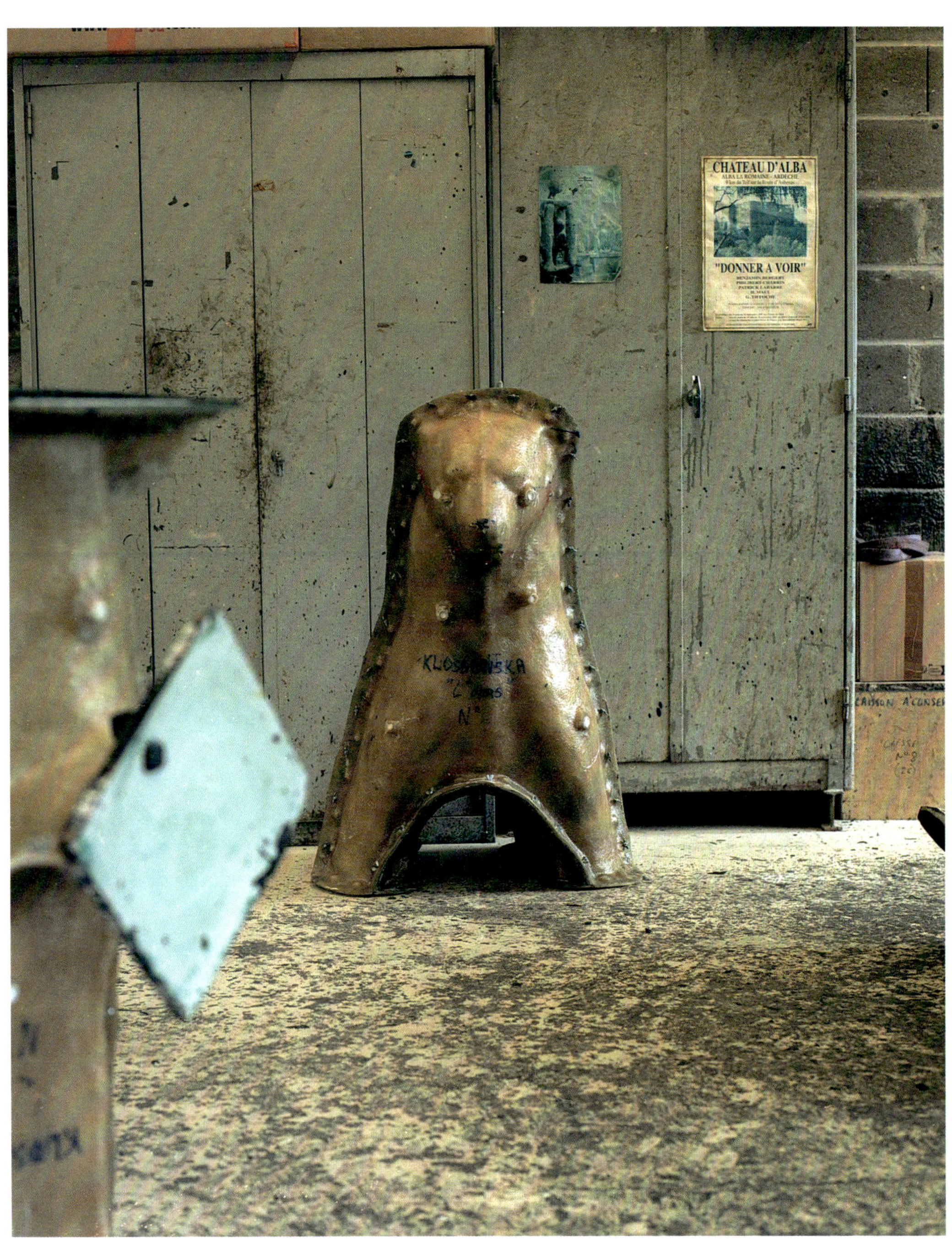
CHATEAU D'ALBA
"DONNER A VOIR"

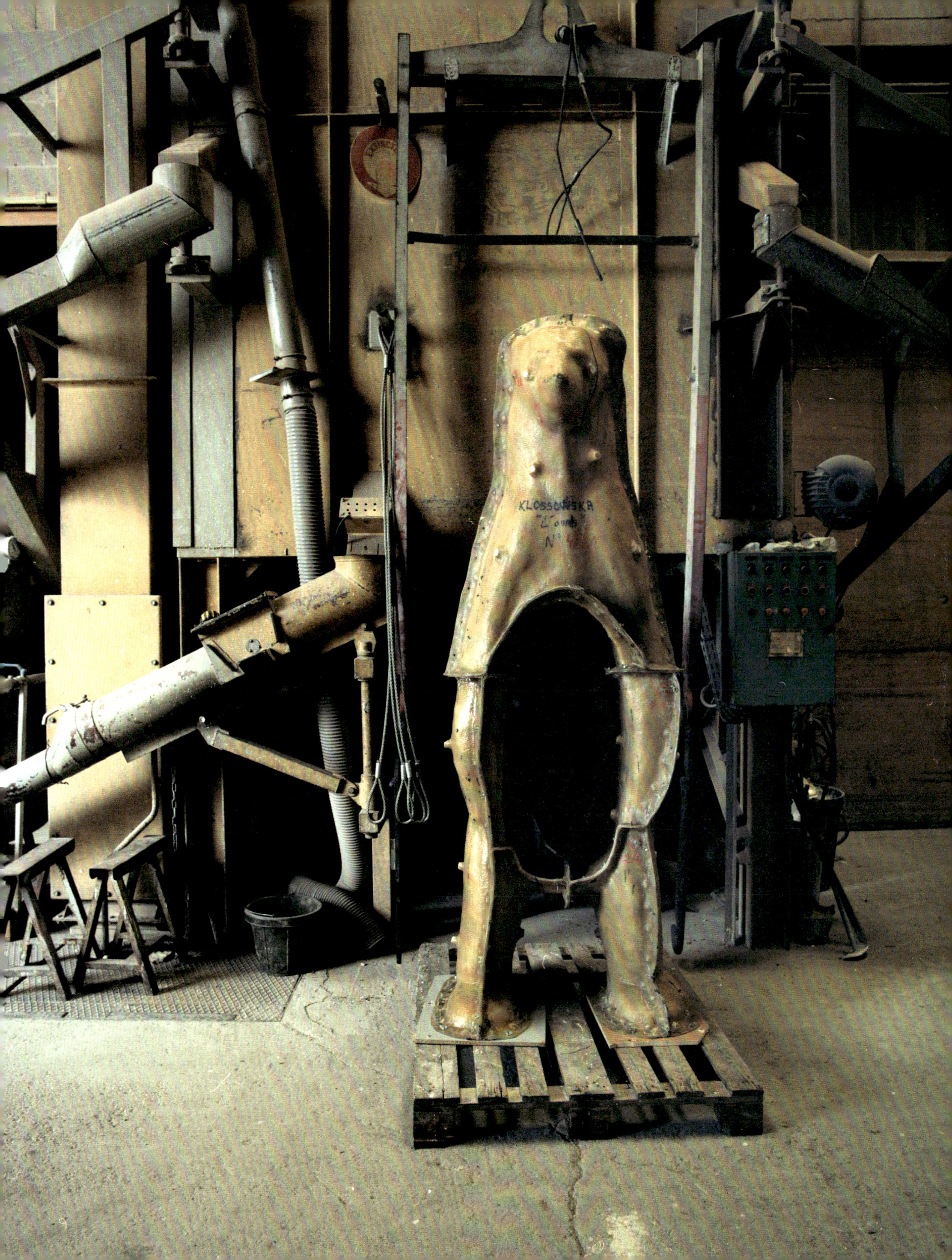
KLOSSOWSKA
"L'ours"

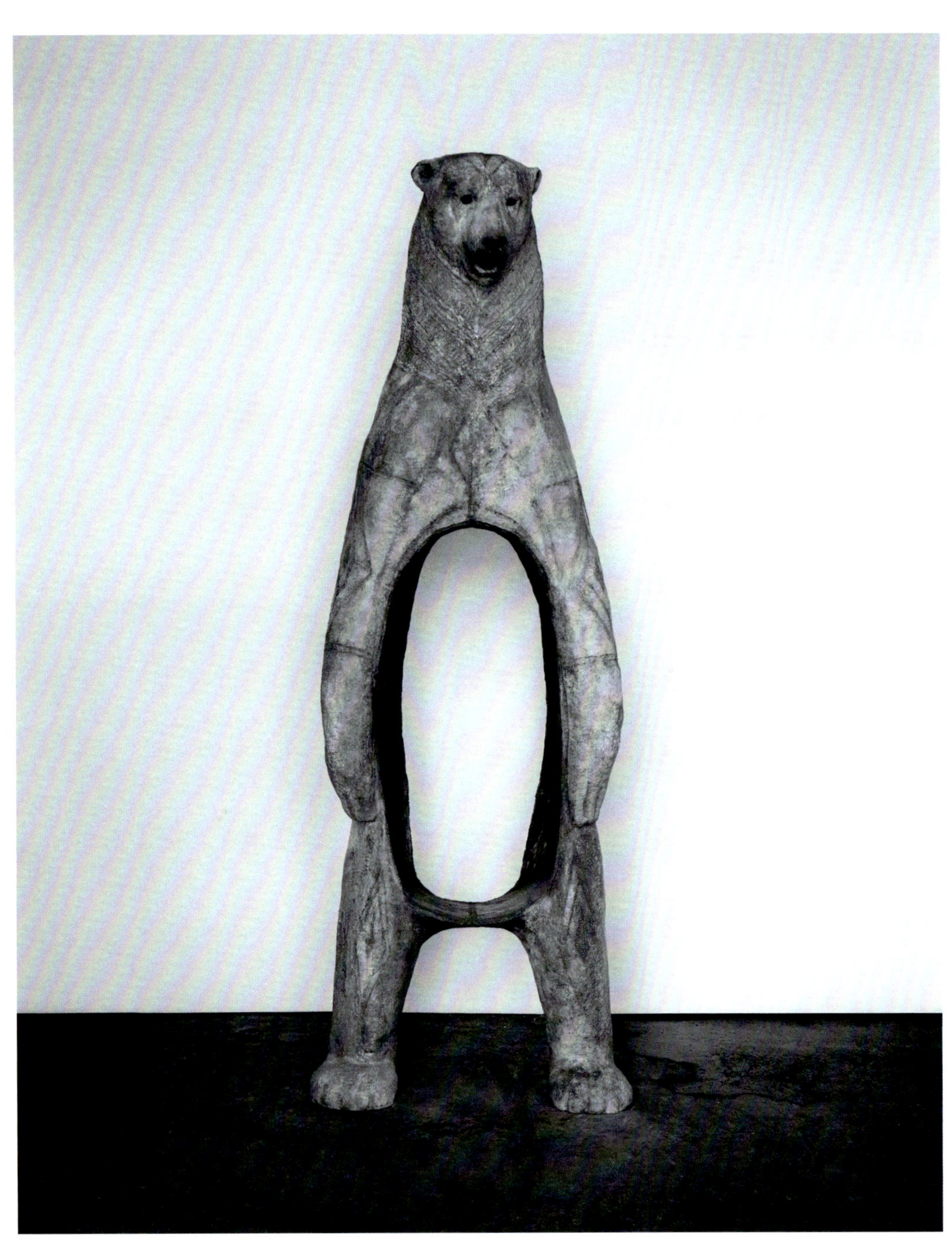

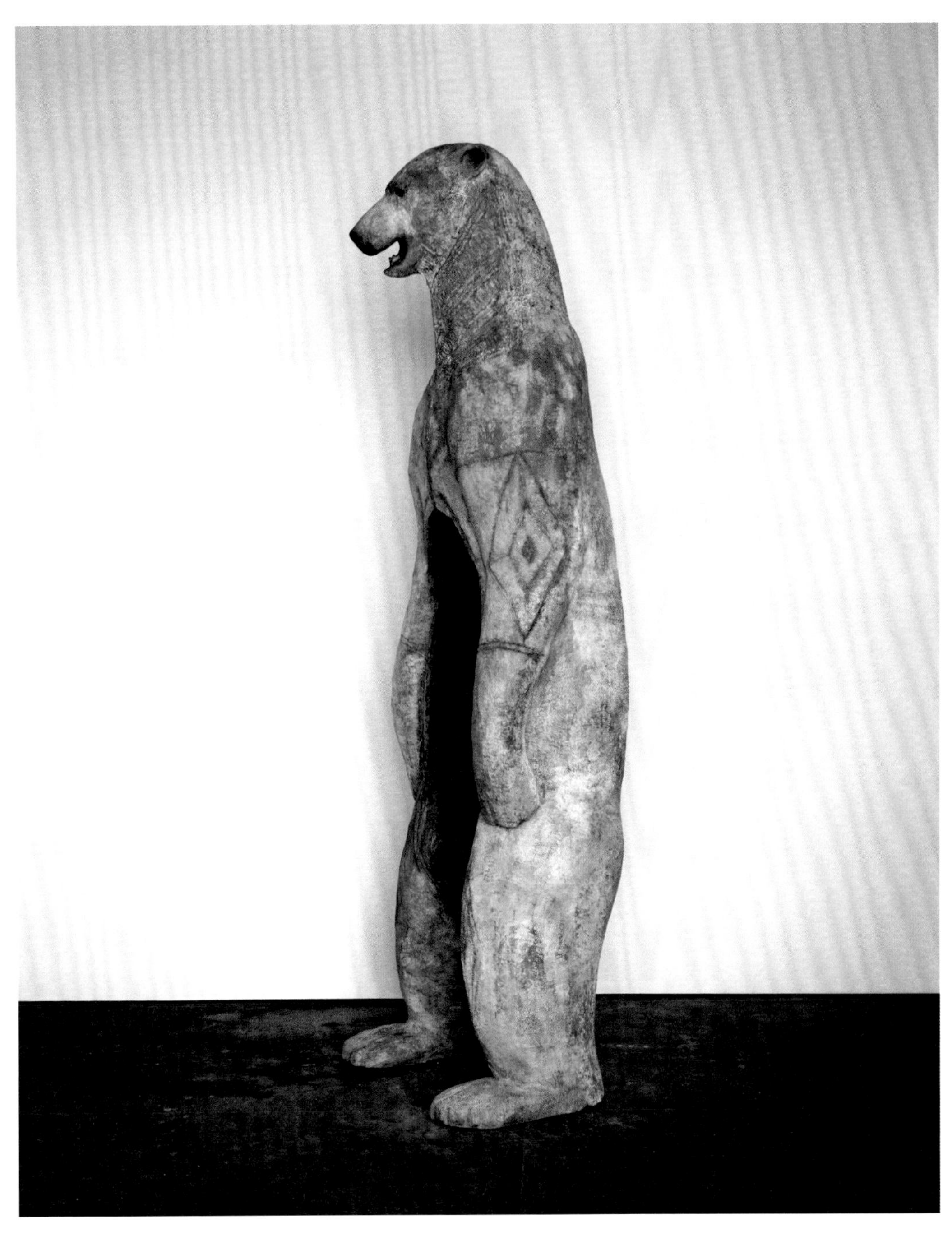

Skops

2024

Bronze

Edition of eight plus one artist's proof

$9^{7}/_{8}$ × 4 inches (25 × 10 cm)

Fonderie de Coubertin, Saint-Rémy-lès-Chevreuse, France

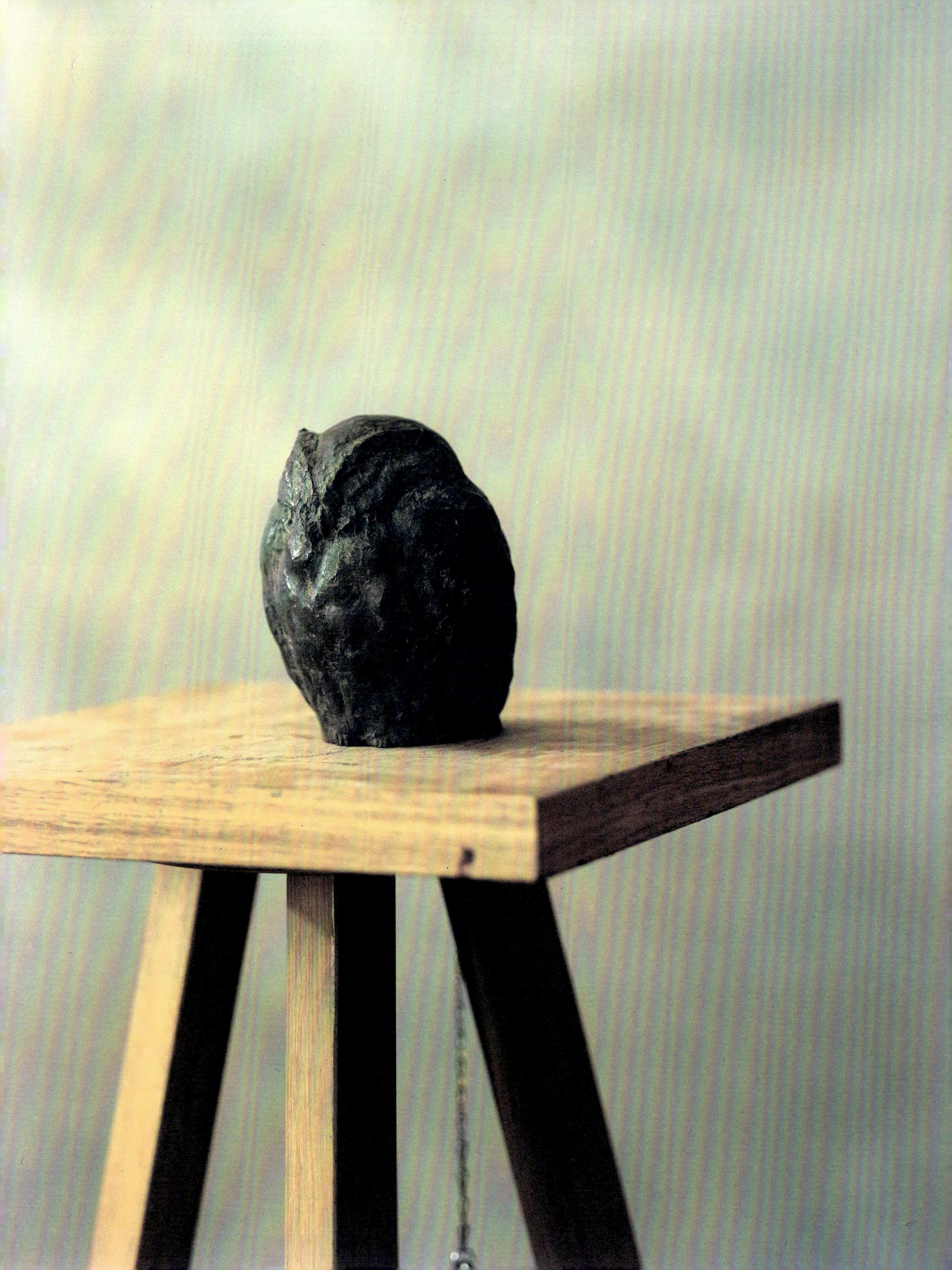

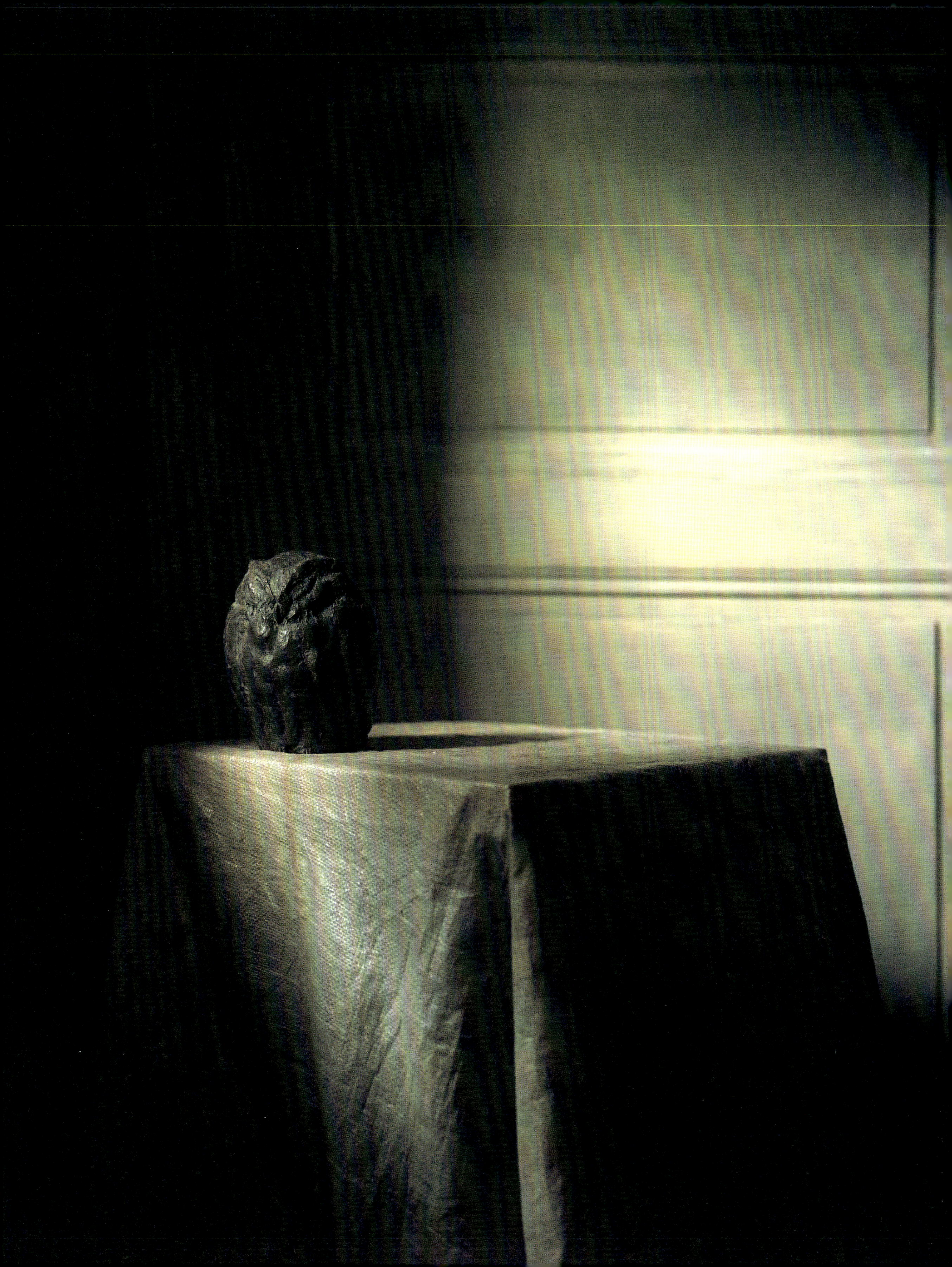

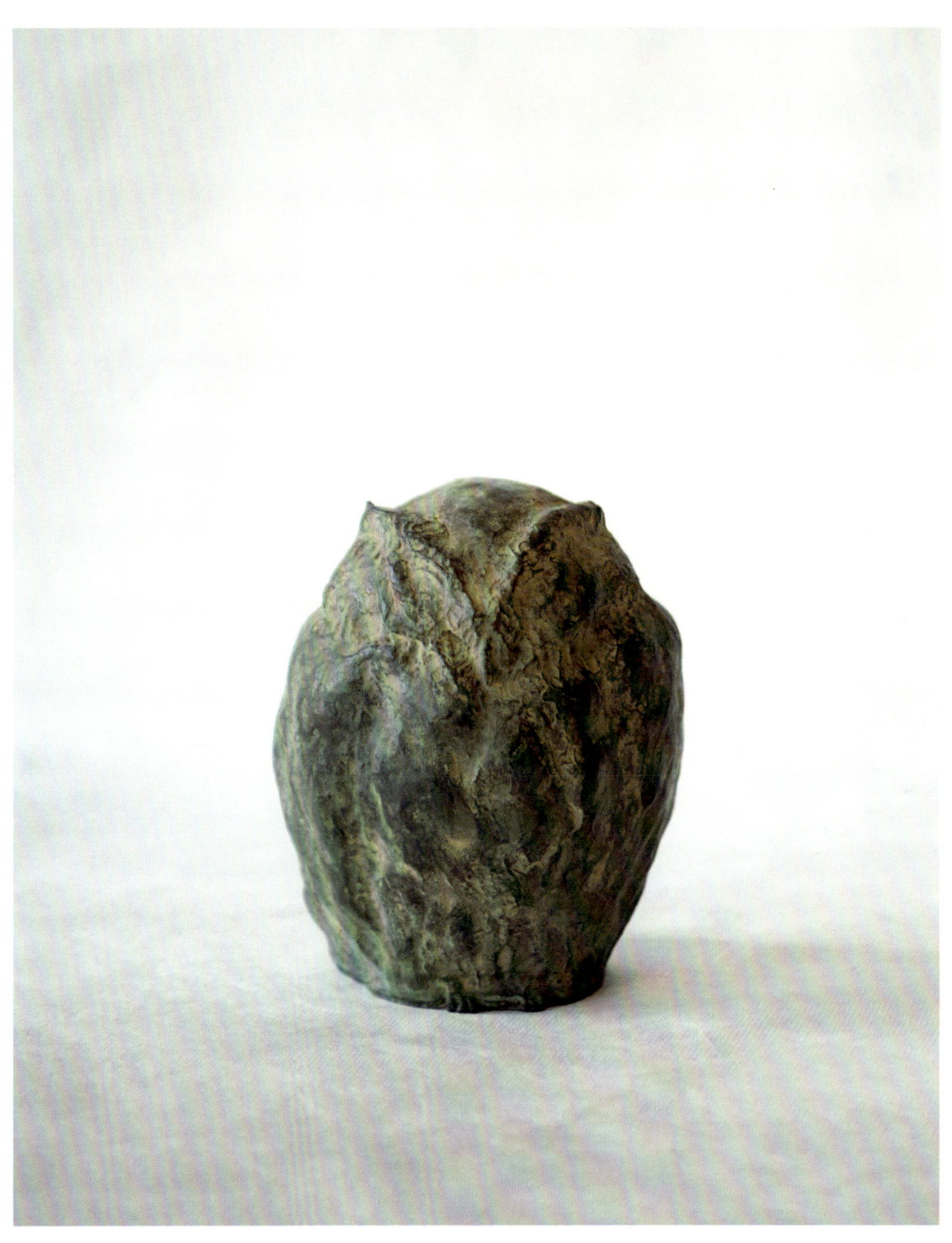

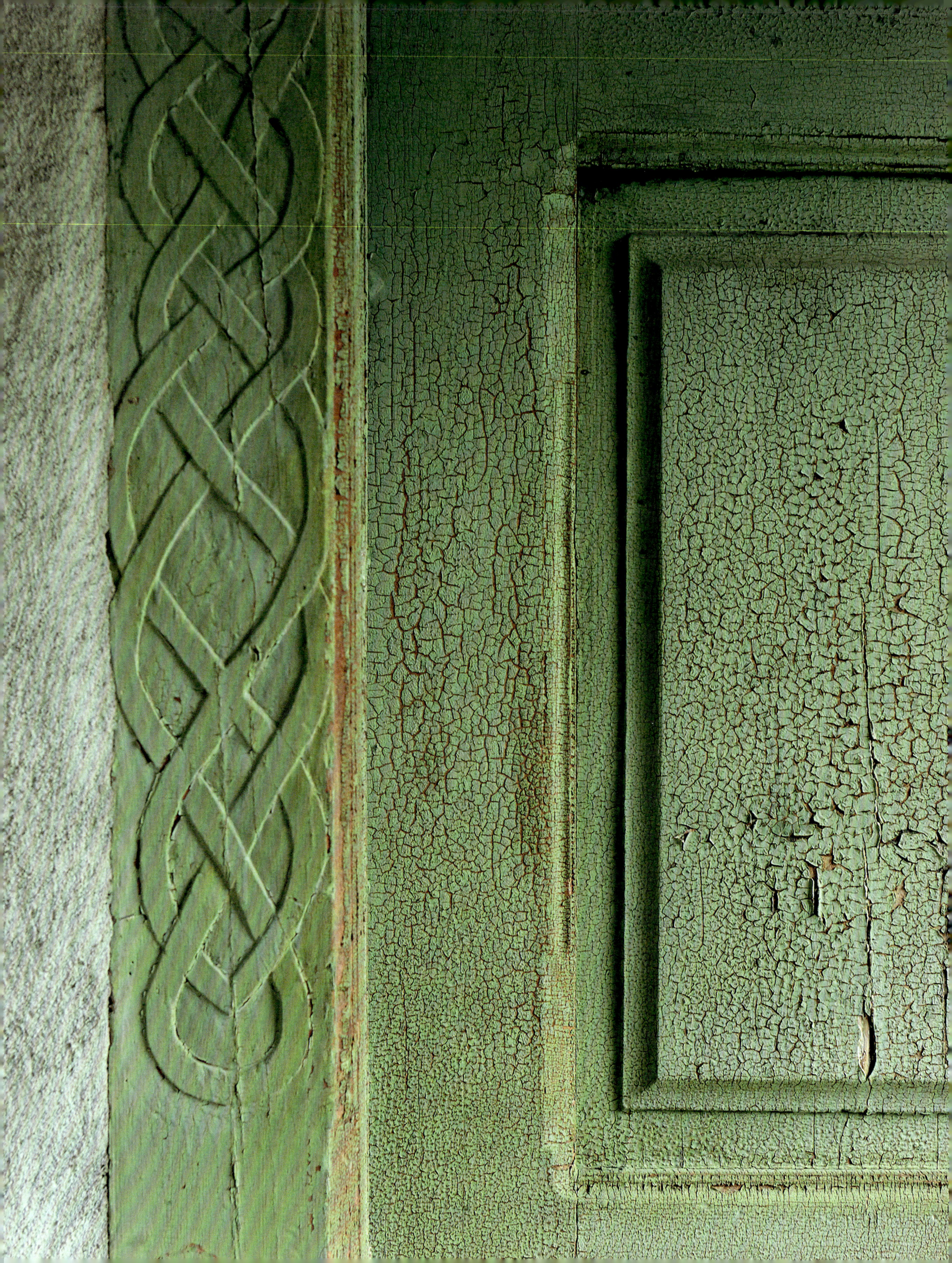

Serpentes
2018

Bronze
Edition of four plus one artist's proof
15 3/4 × 9 7/8 × 26 3/8 inches (40 × 25.1 × 67 cm)
Fonderie Patrick Laroche, Paris

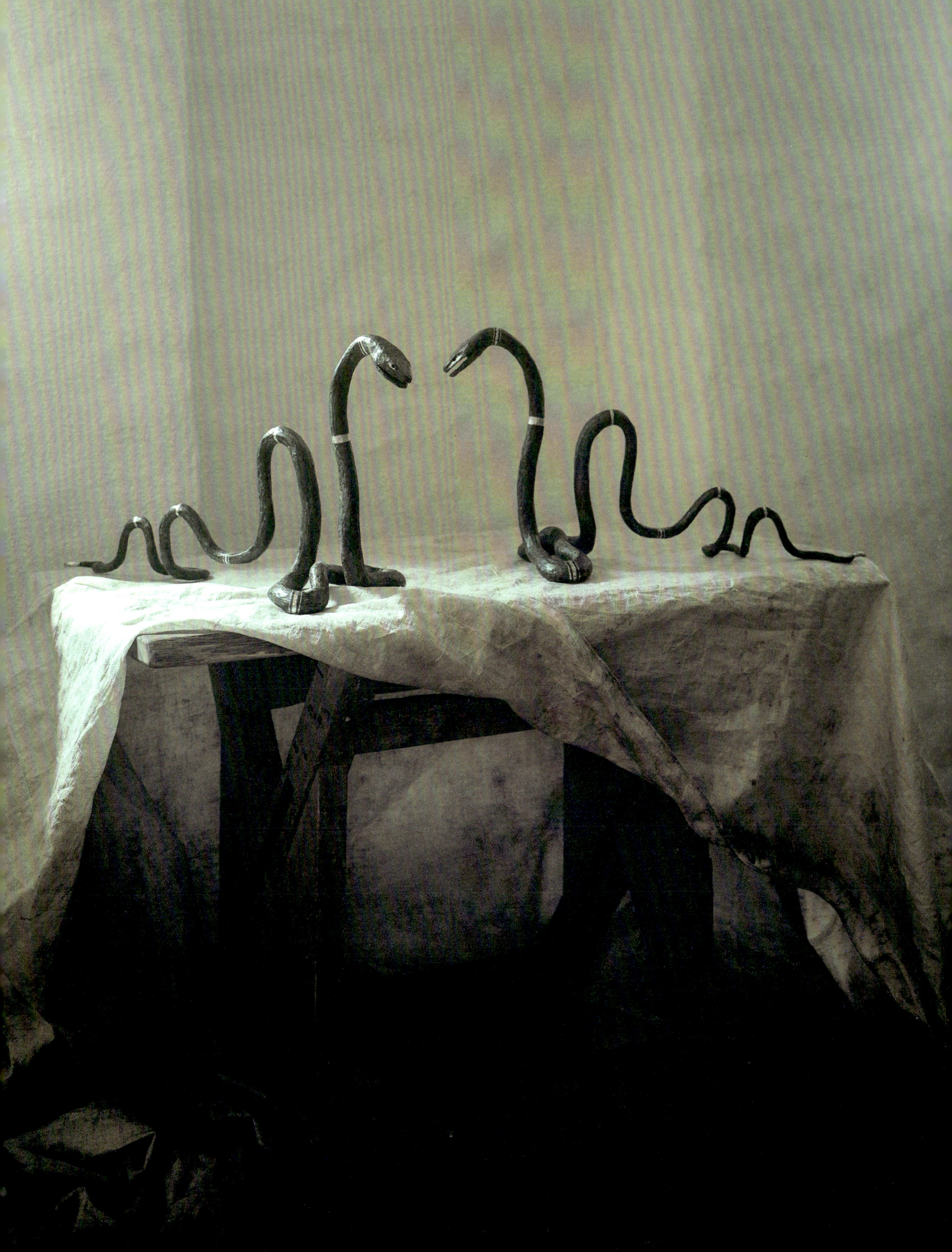

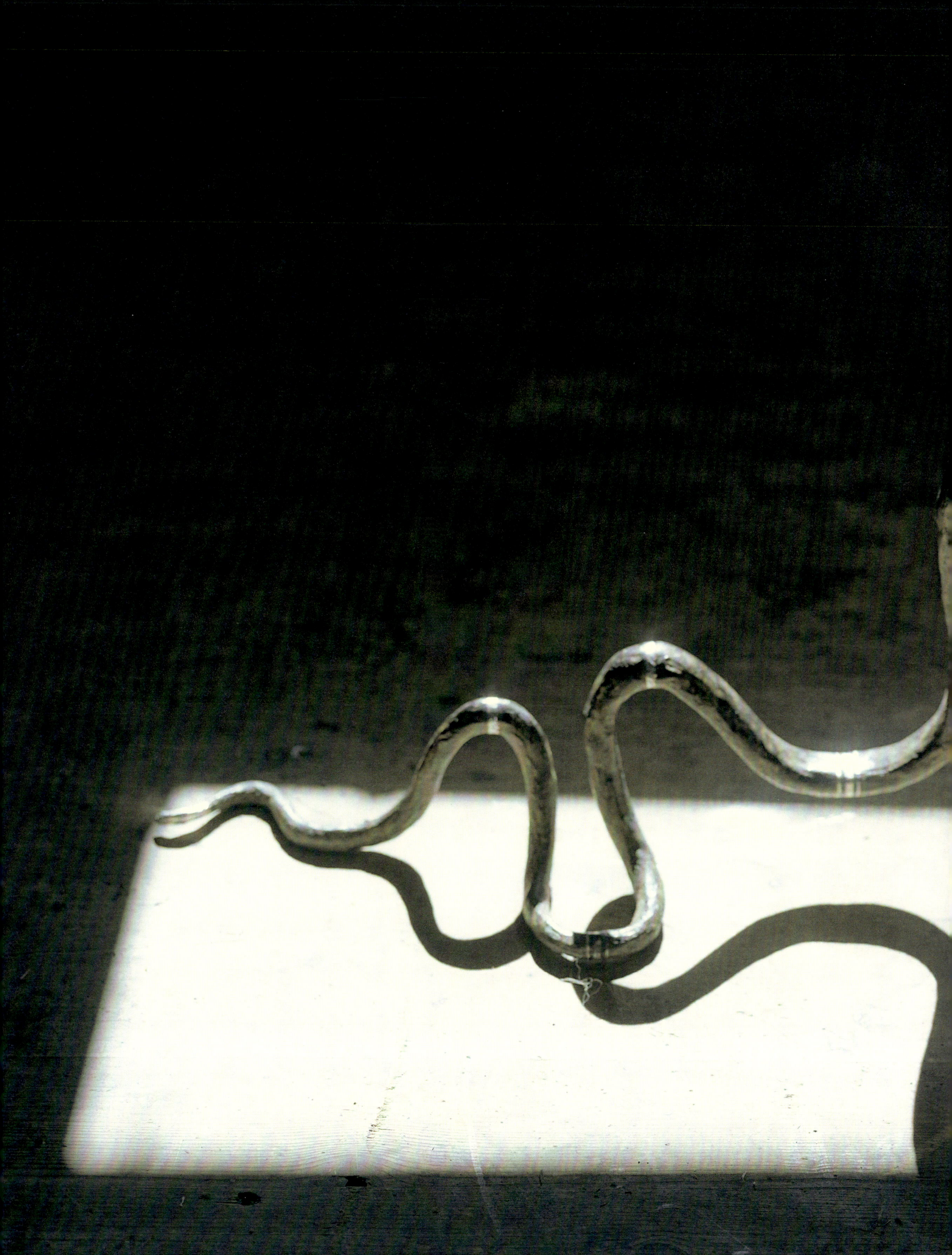

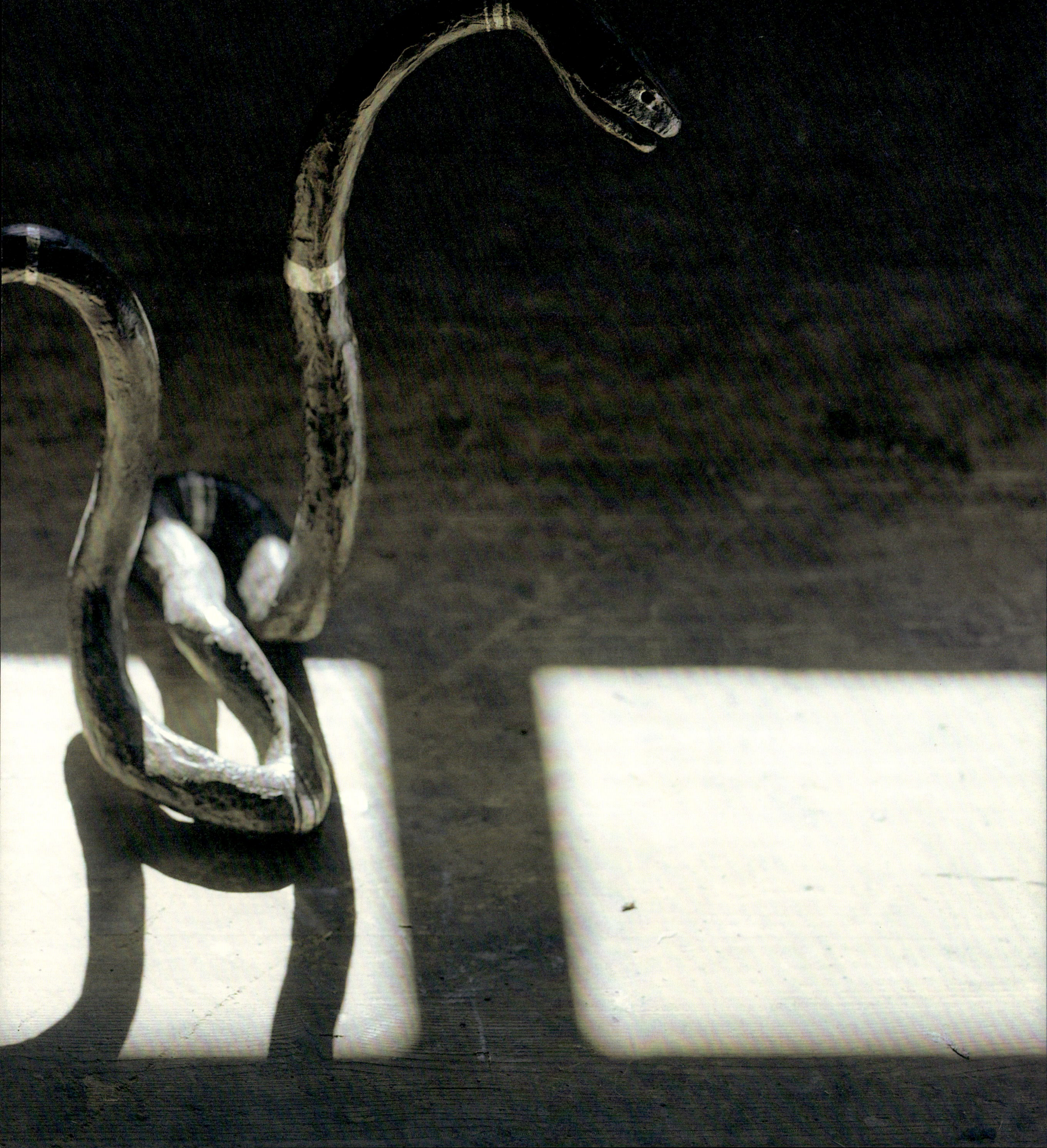

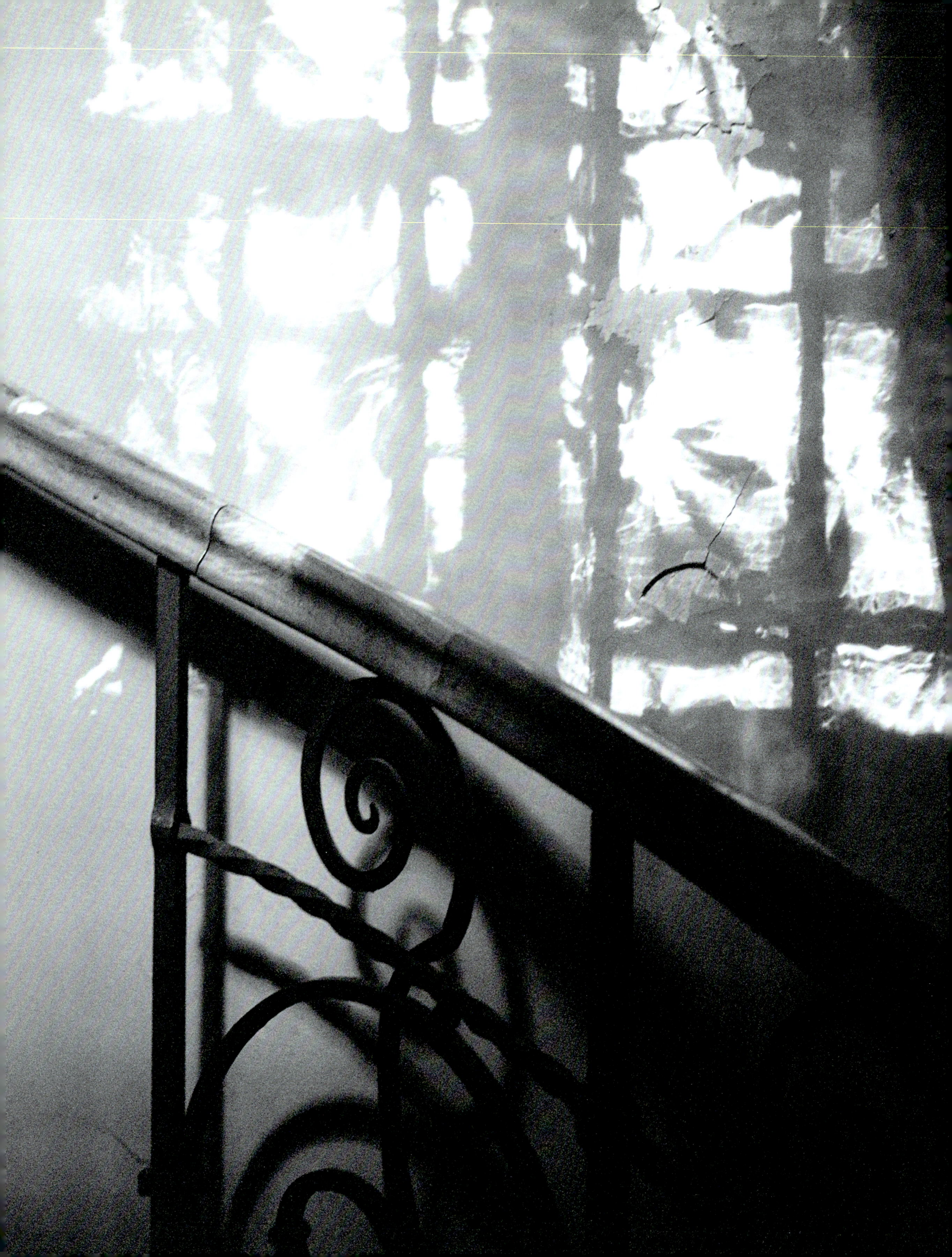

Small Tree with Owl

2024

Bronze
Edition of eight plus two artist's proofs
21 × 10 1/4 × 14 1/8 inches (53.5 × 26 × 36 cm)
Fonderie de Coubertin, Saint-Rémy-lès-Chevreuse, France

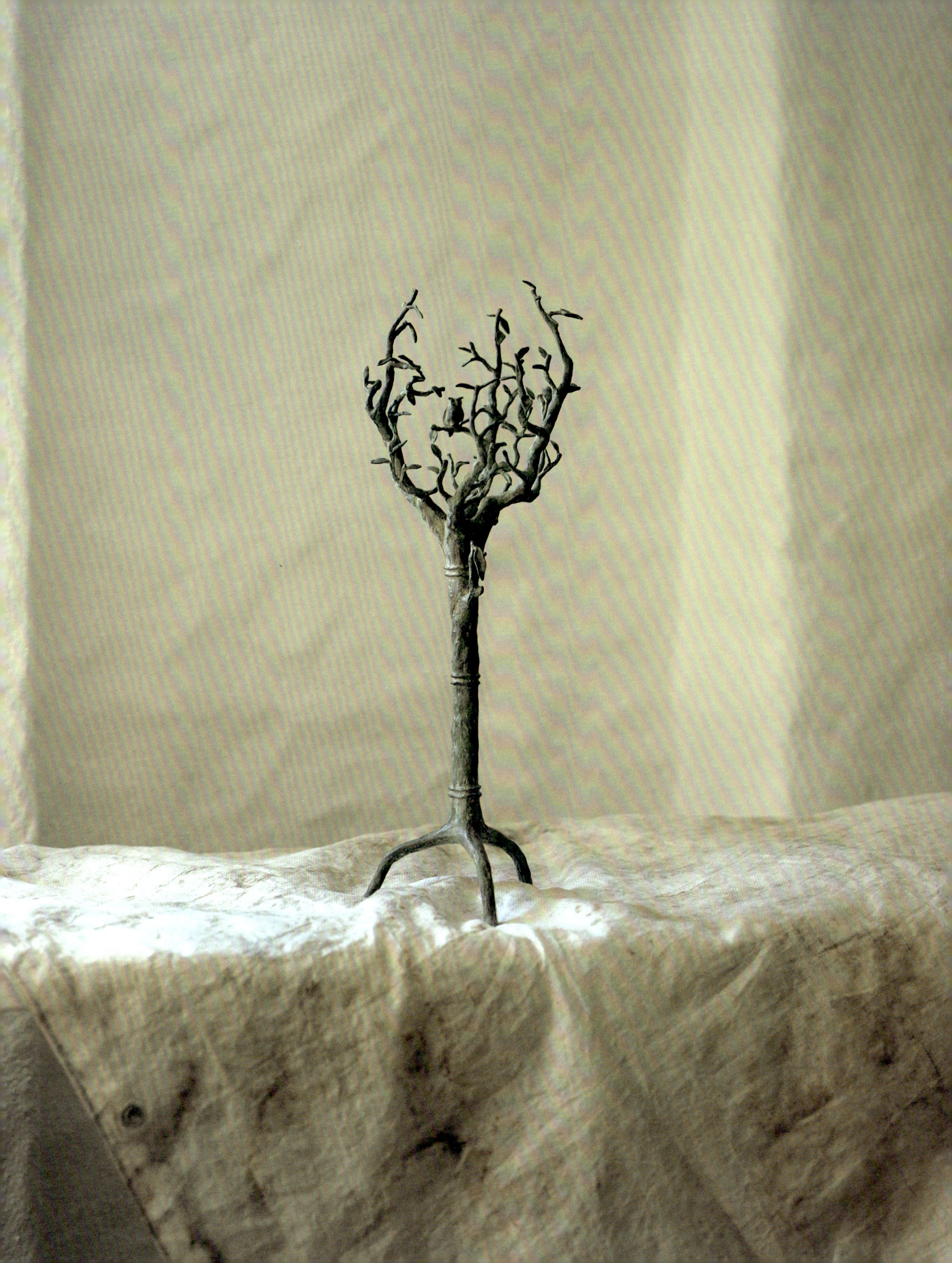

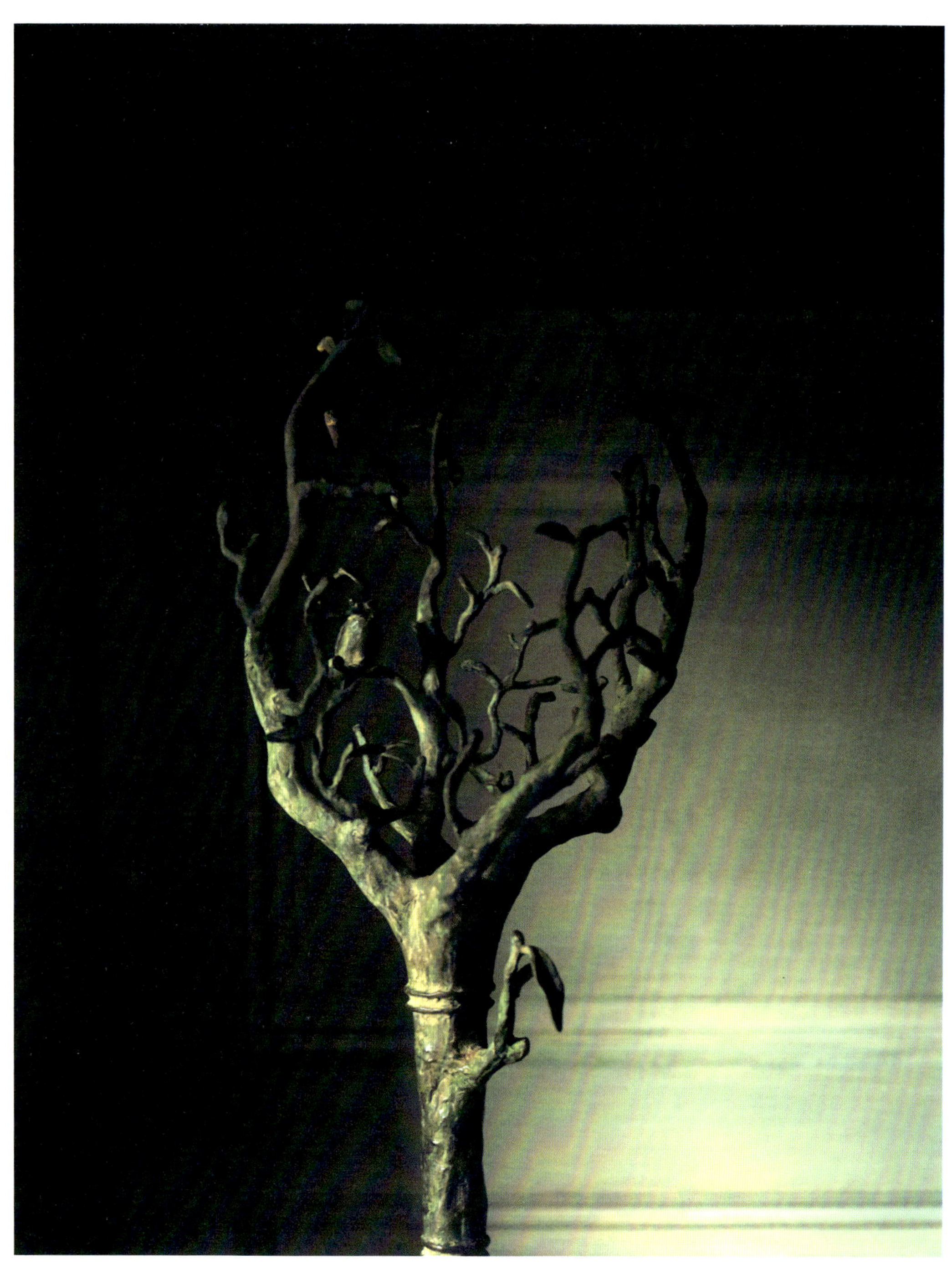

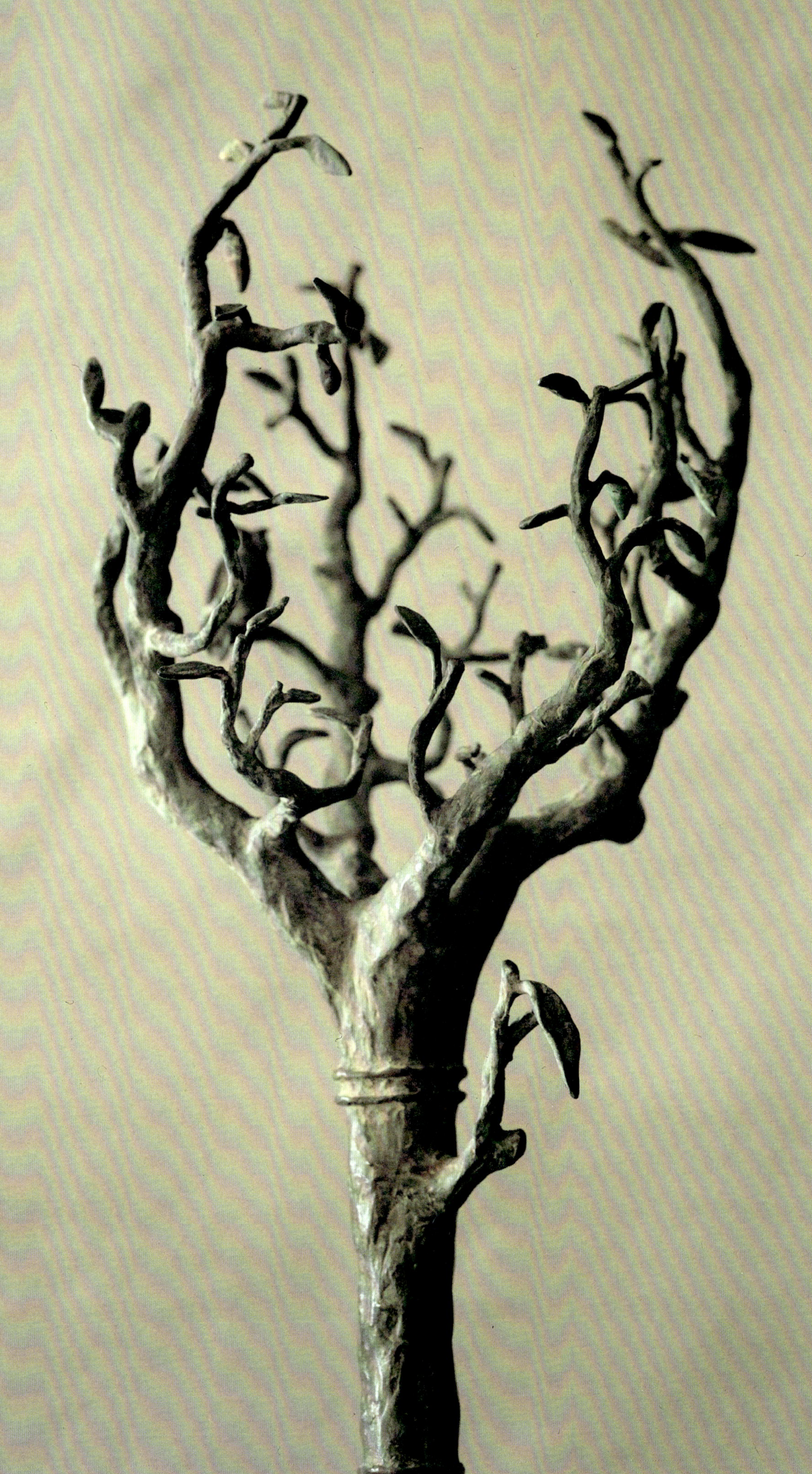

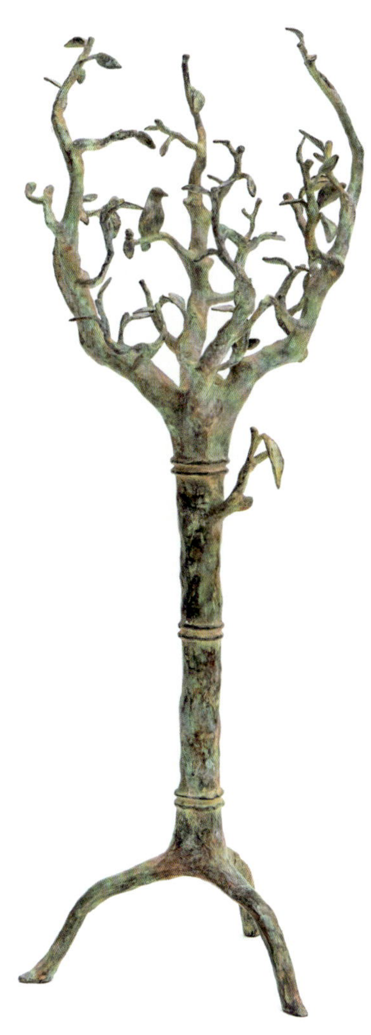

Sobek

2018

Bronze

Edition of three plus one artist's proof

$16\,{}^{7}/_{8} \times 21\,{}^{5}/_{8} \times 81\,{}^{1}/_{8}$ inches (43 × 55 × 206 cm)

Fonderie Patrick Laroche, Paris

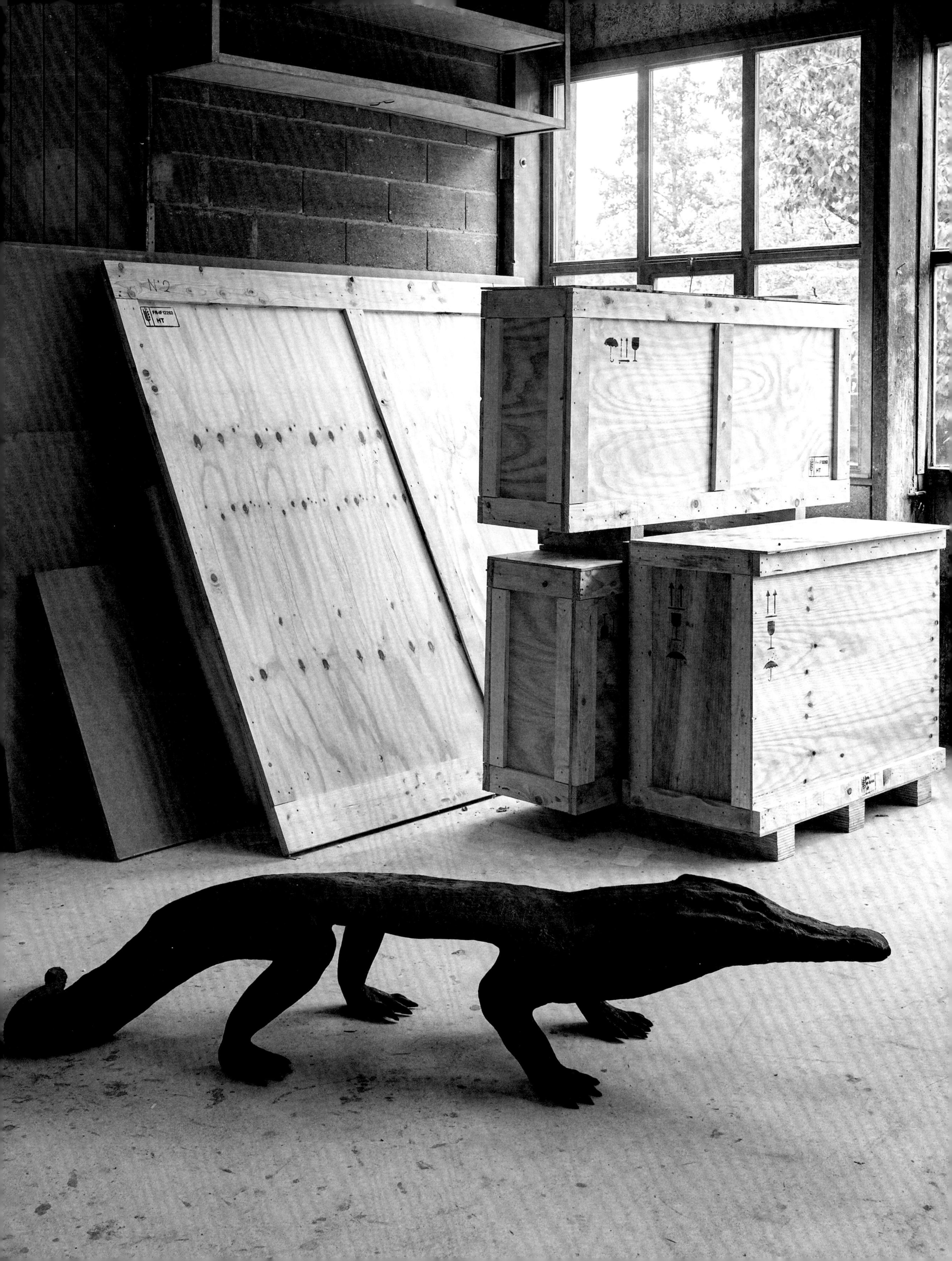
N°2
HT

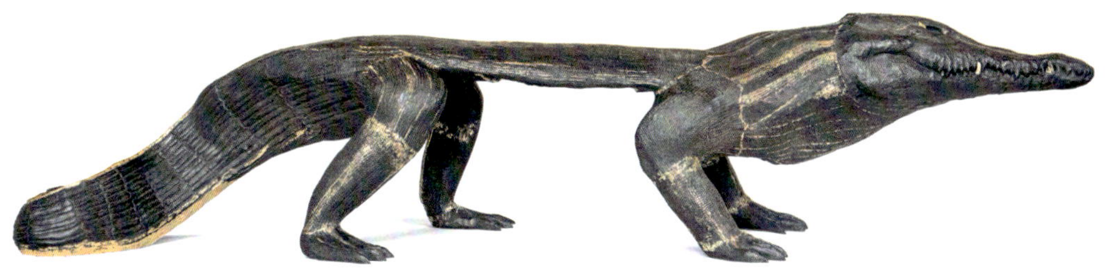

Wood Pile / Misty Swamp

2022

Screen: sipo wood, platinum, palladium, gold leaf and oil paint

Unique

88 5/8 × 97 5/8 × 3/4 inches (225 × 248 × 2 cm)

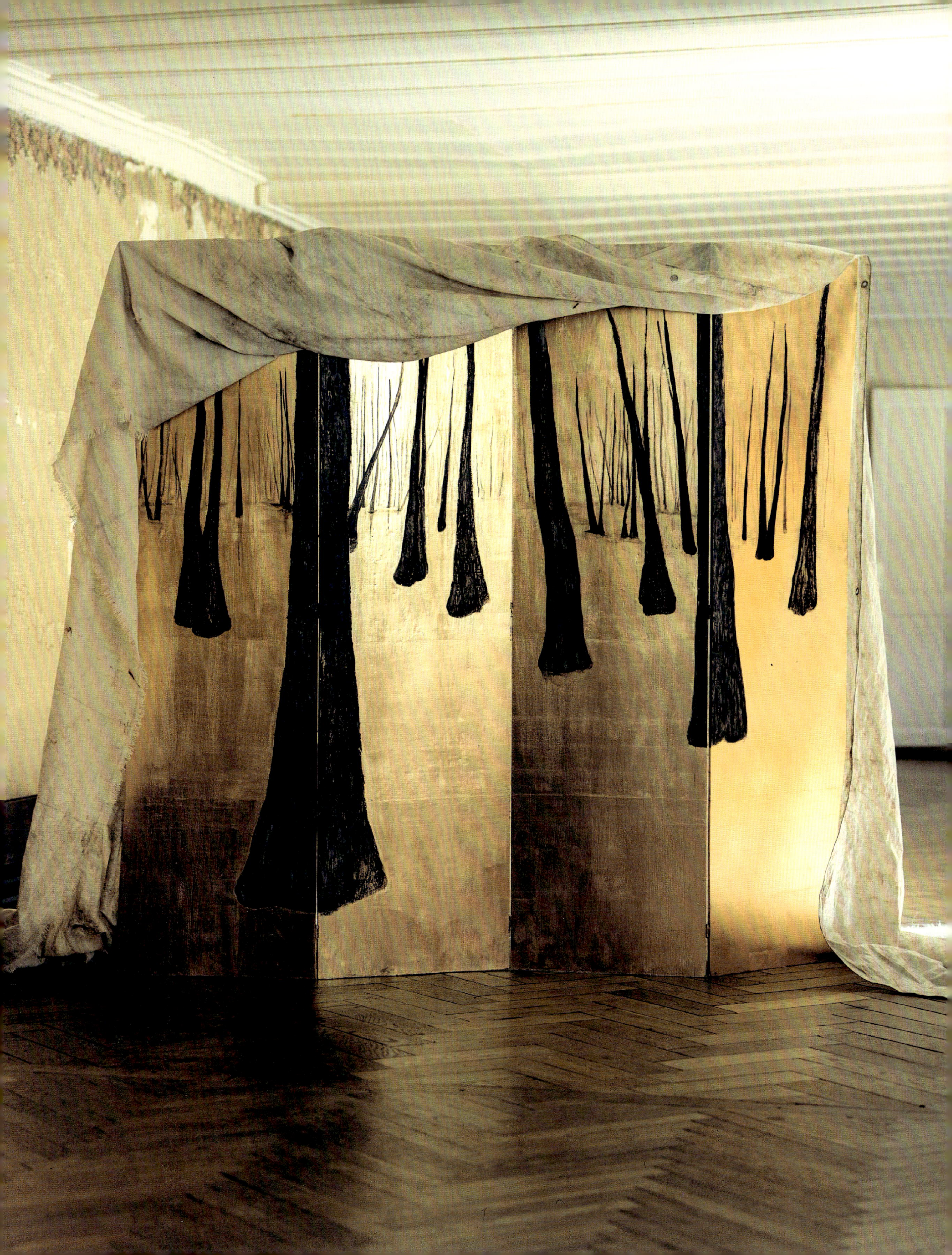

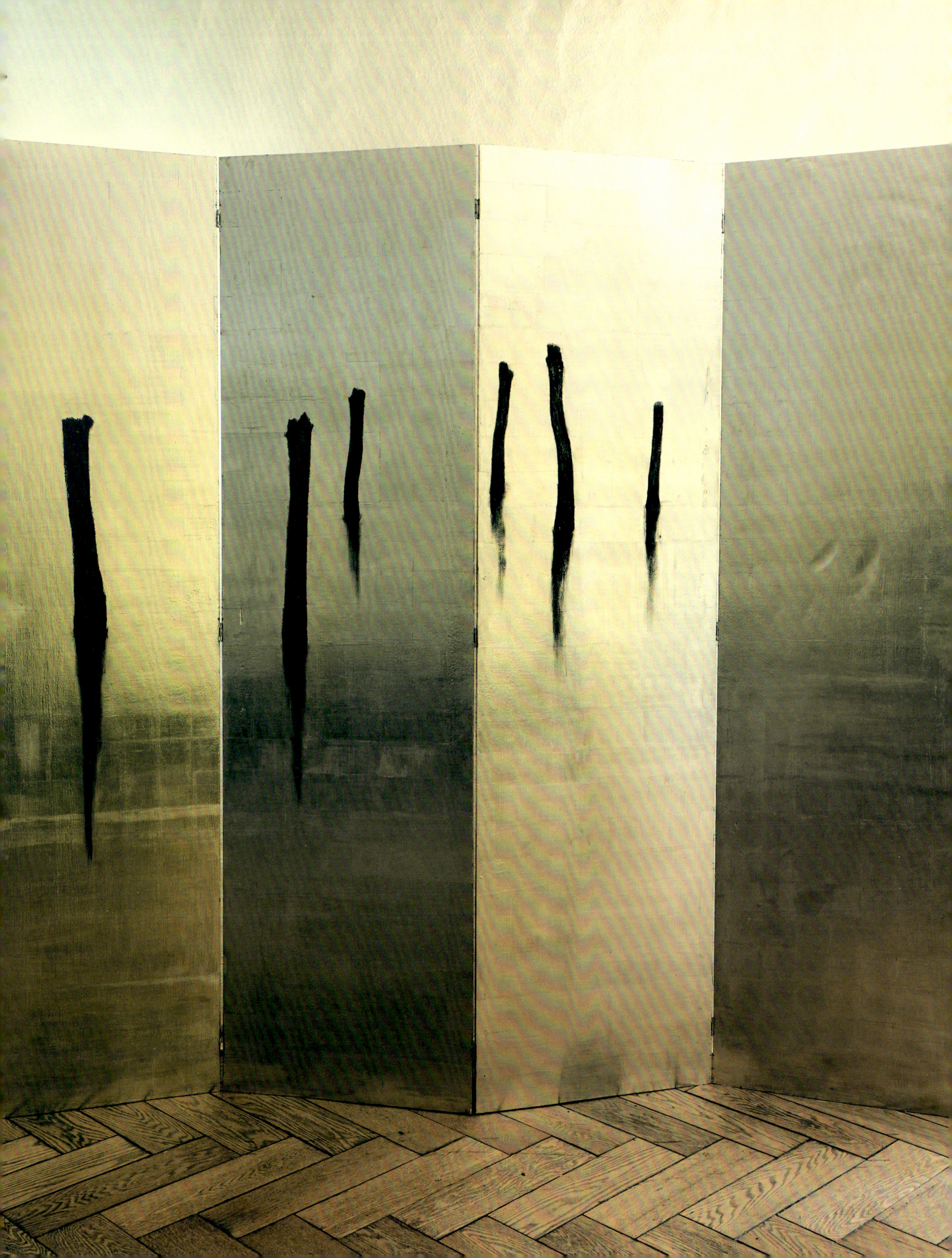

Wepwawet

2022

Bronze

Edition of eight plus two artist's proofs

$29\,^1/_2 \times 11\,^3/_4 \times 57\,^1/_2$ inches (75 × 30 × 146 cm)

Fonderie de Coubertin, Saint-Rémy-lès-Chevreuse, France

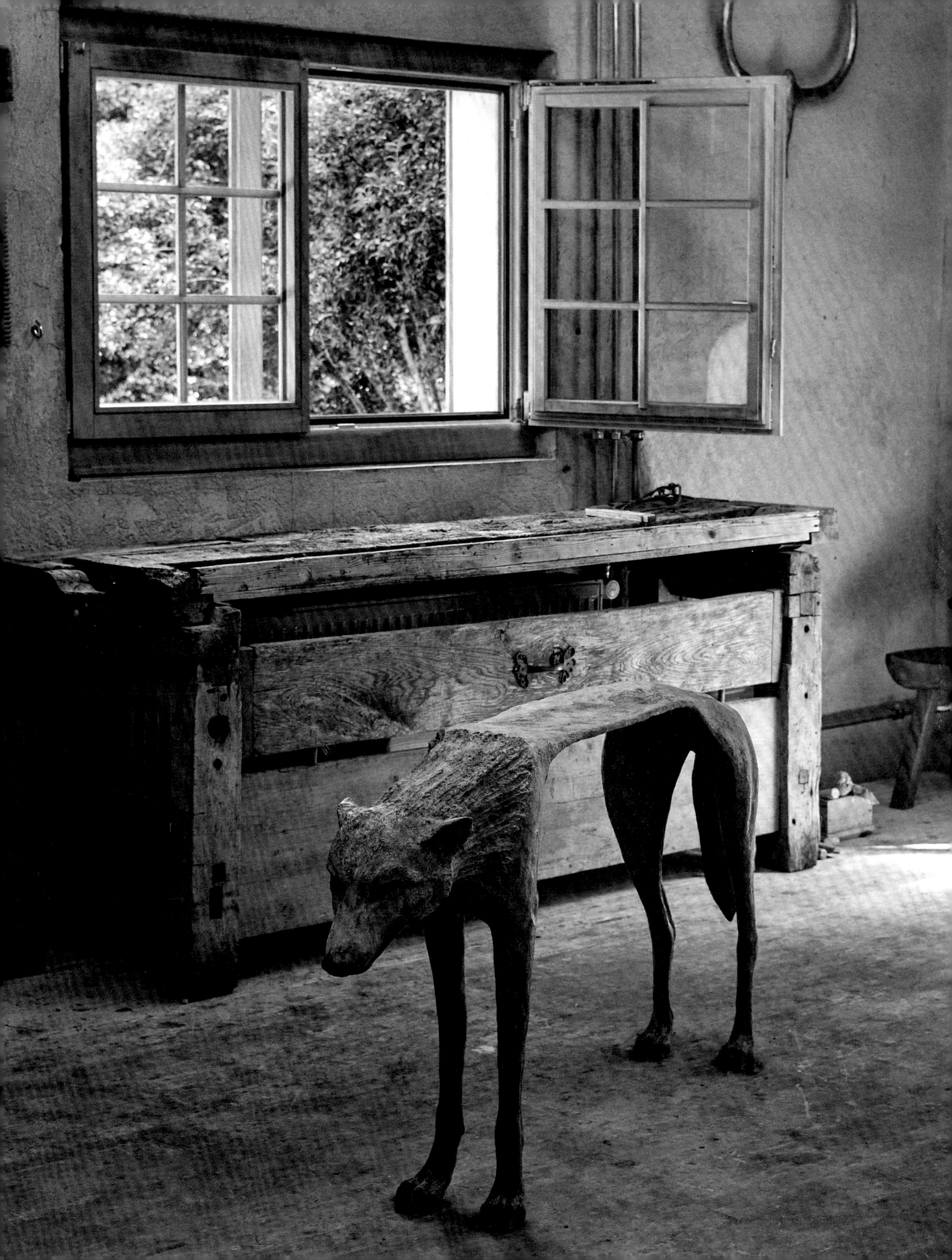

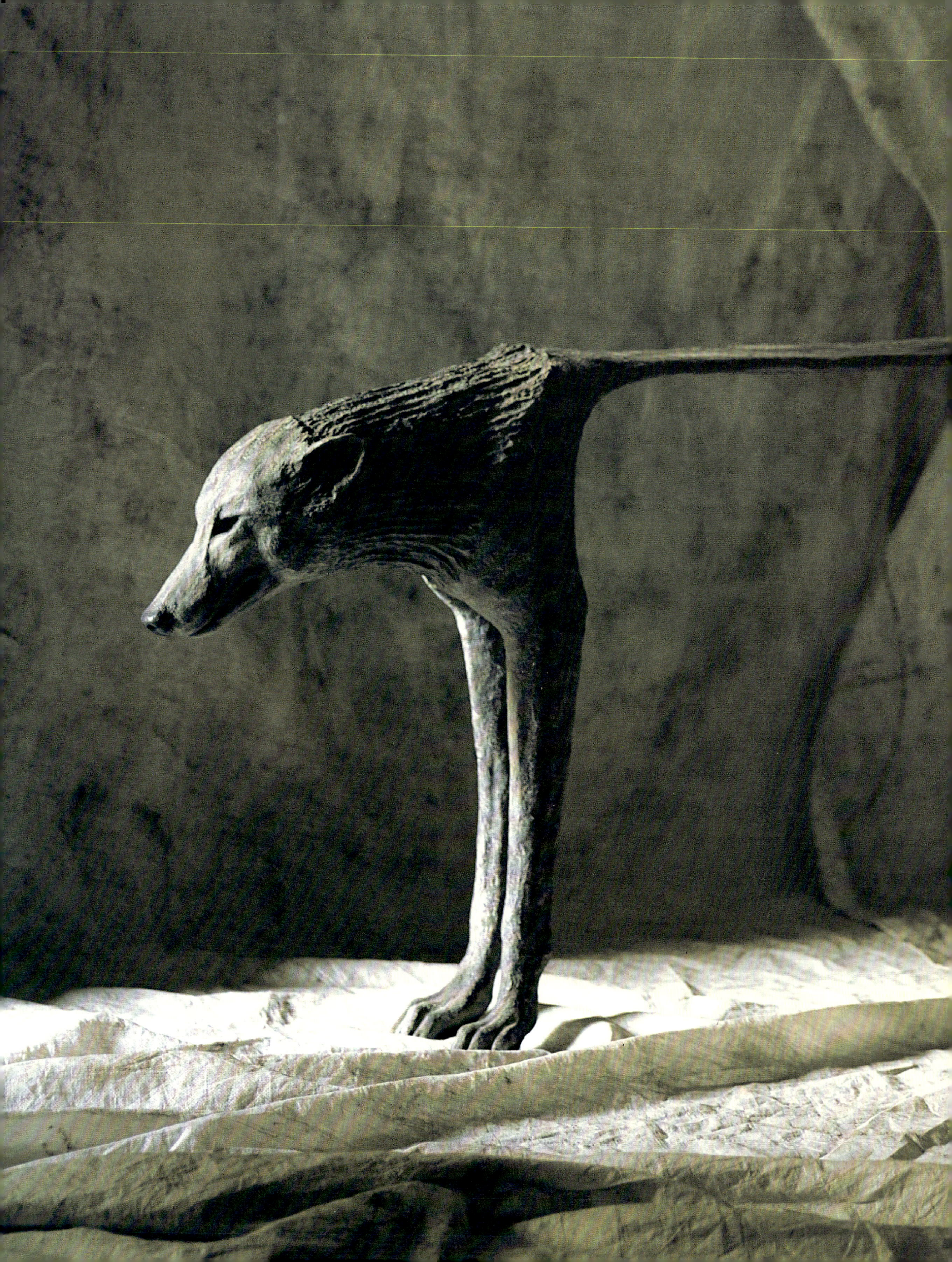

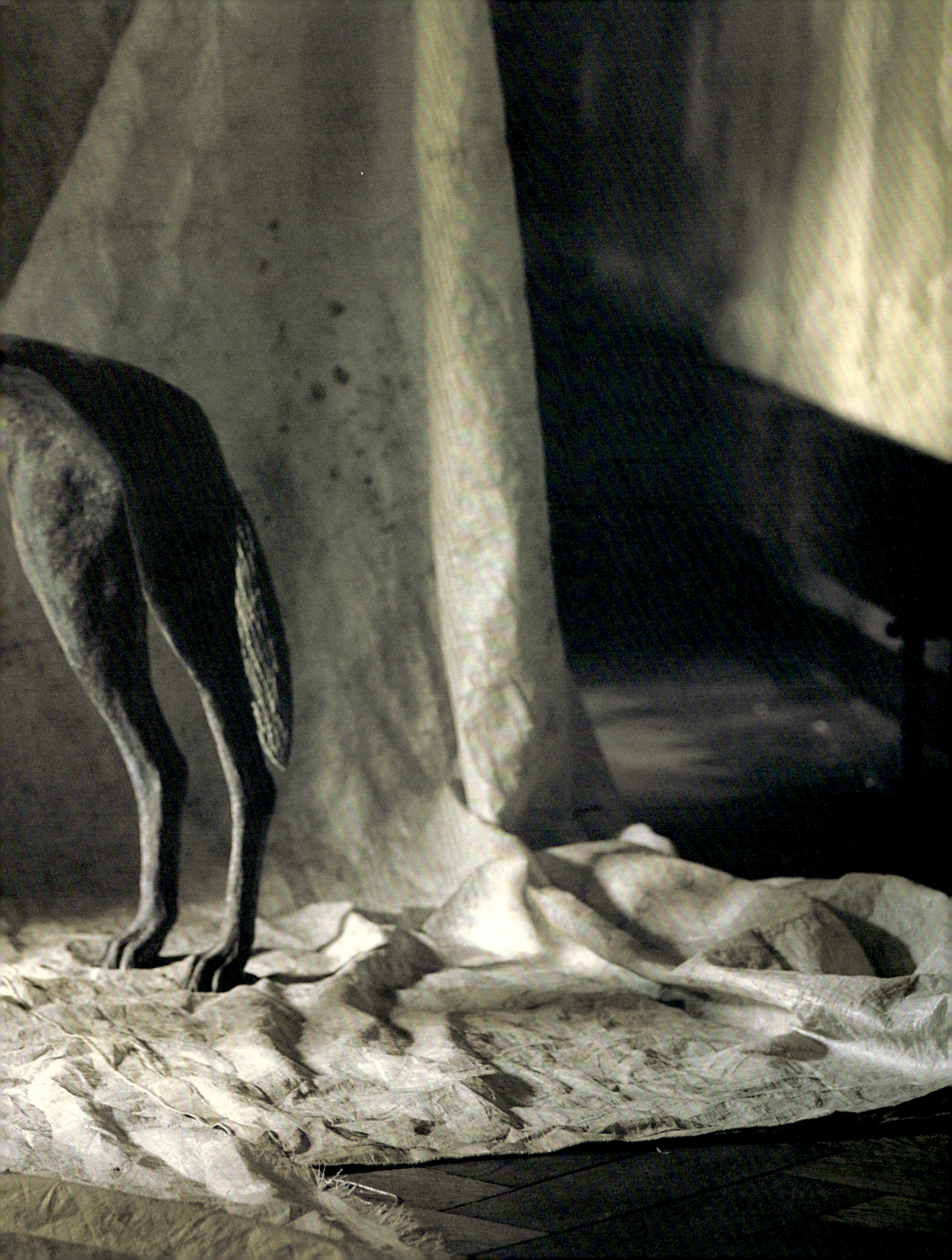

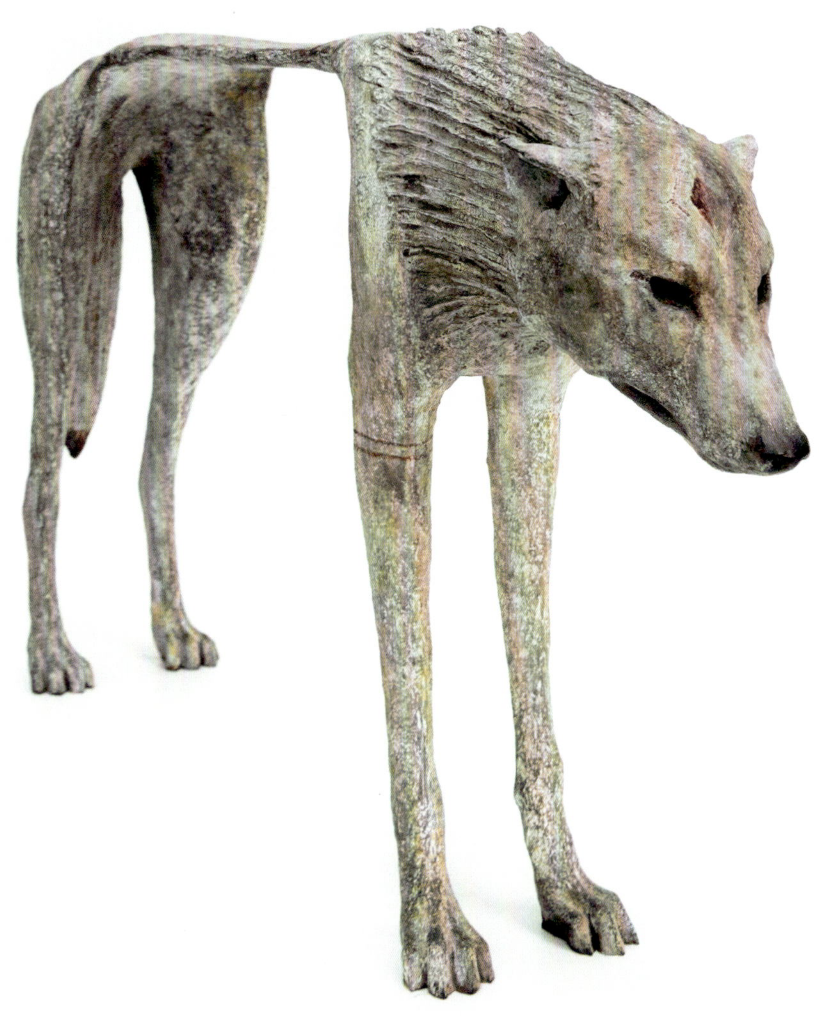

Lakshmi

2022

Bronze

Edition of eight plus four artist's proofs

$15\,^{3}/_{8} \times 5\,^{7}/_{8} \times 9$ inches ($39 \times 15 \times 23$ cm)

Fonderie de Coubertin, Saint-Rémy-lès-Chevreuse, France

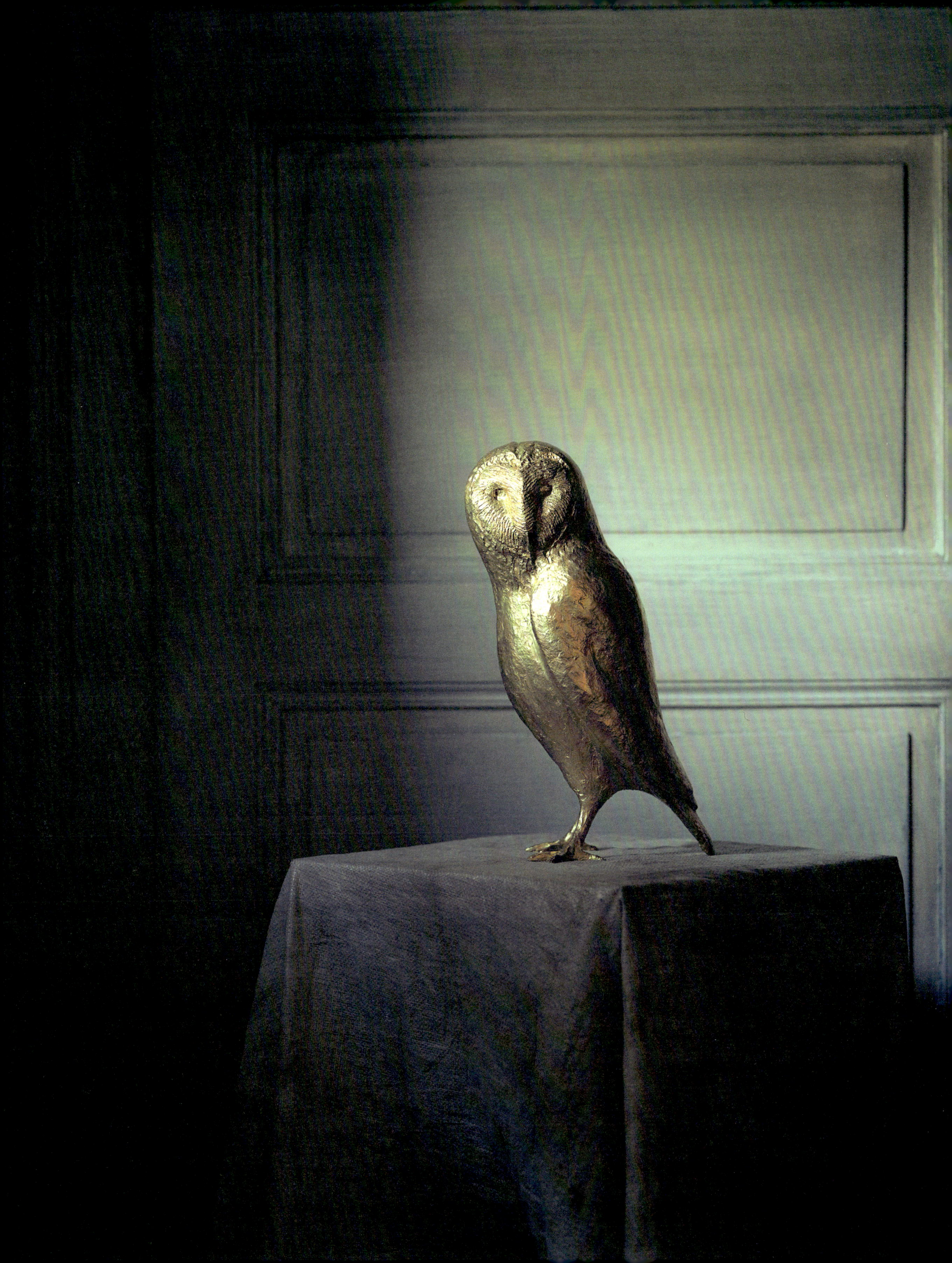

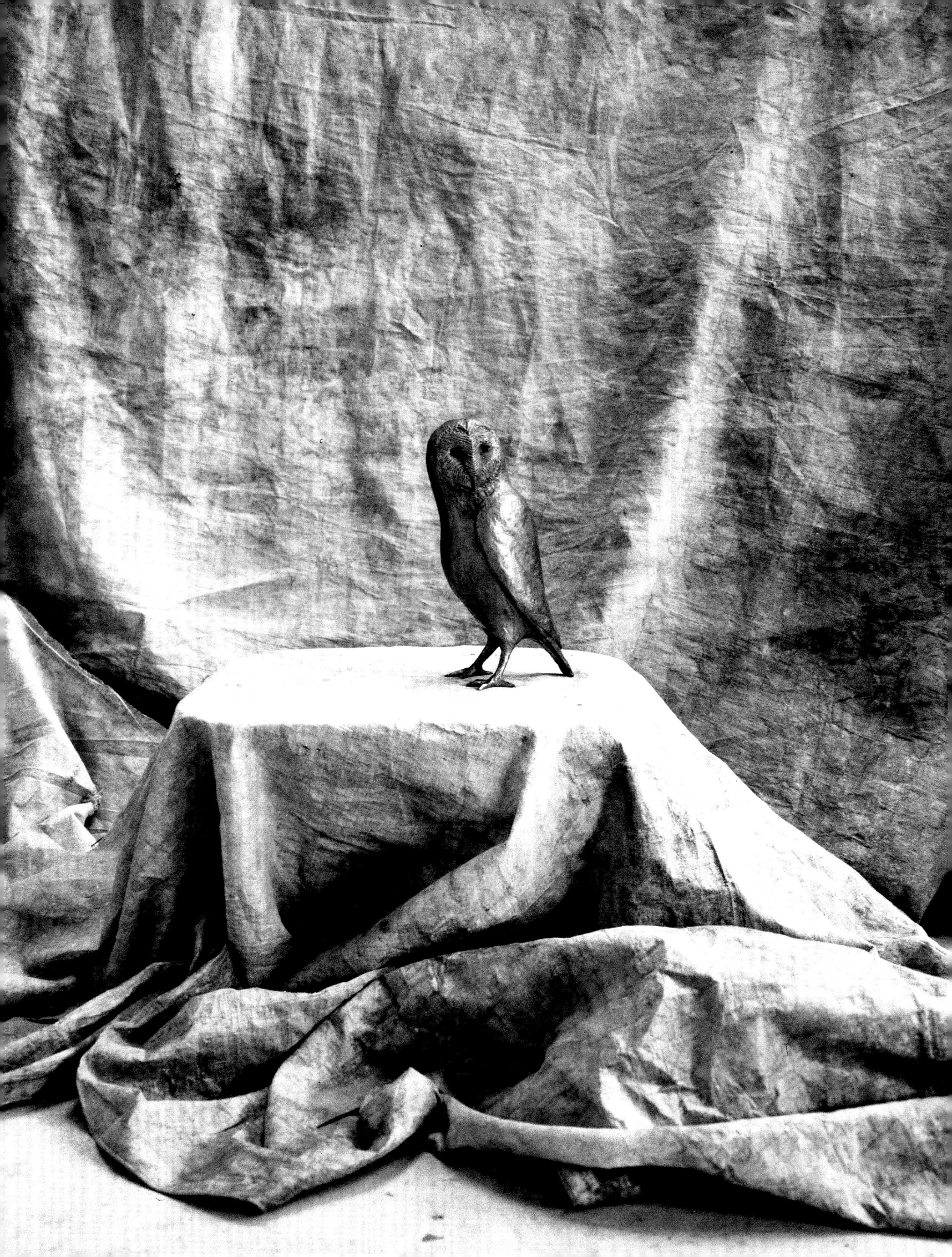

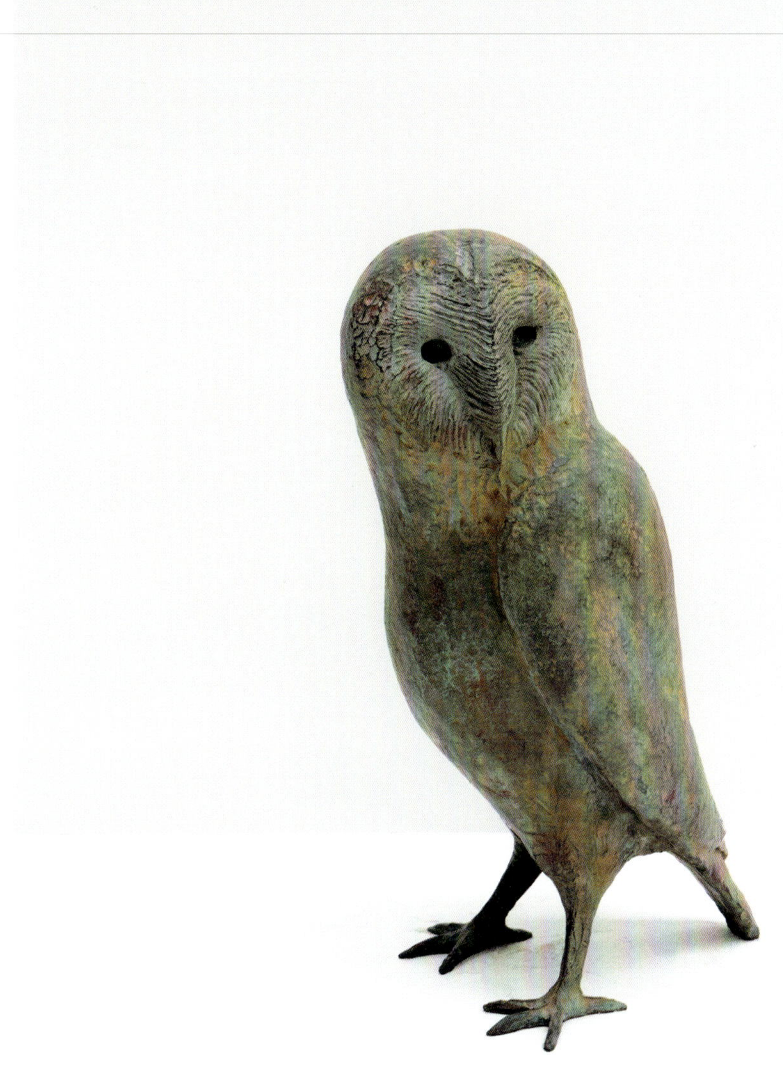

Bird on a Pond

2024

Rosewood with bronze

Unique

22 1/2 × 24 × 26 3/4 inches (57 × 61 × 68 cm)

Fonderie de Coubertin, Saint-Rémy-lès-Chevreuse, France

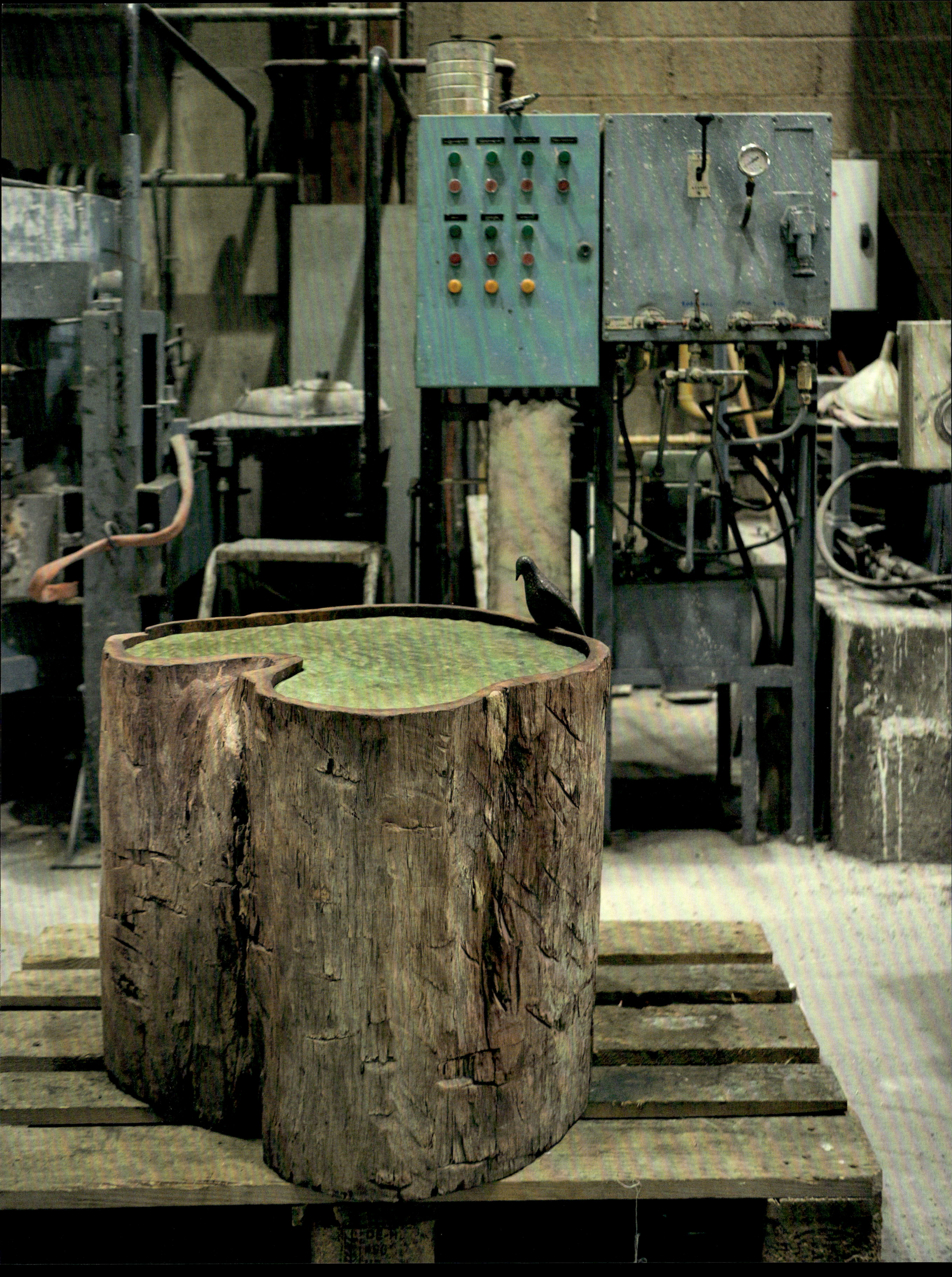

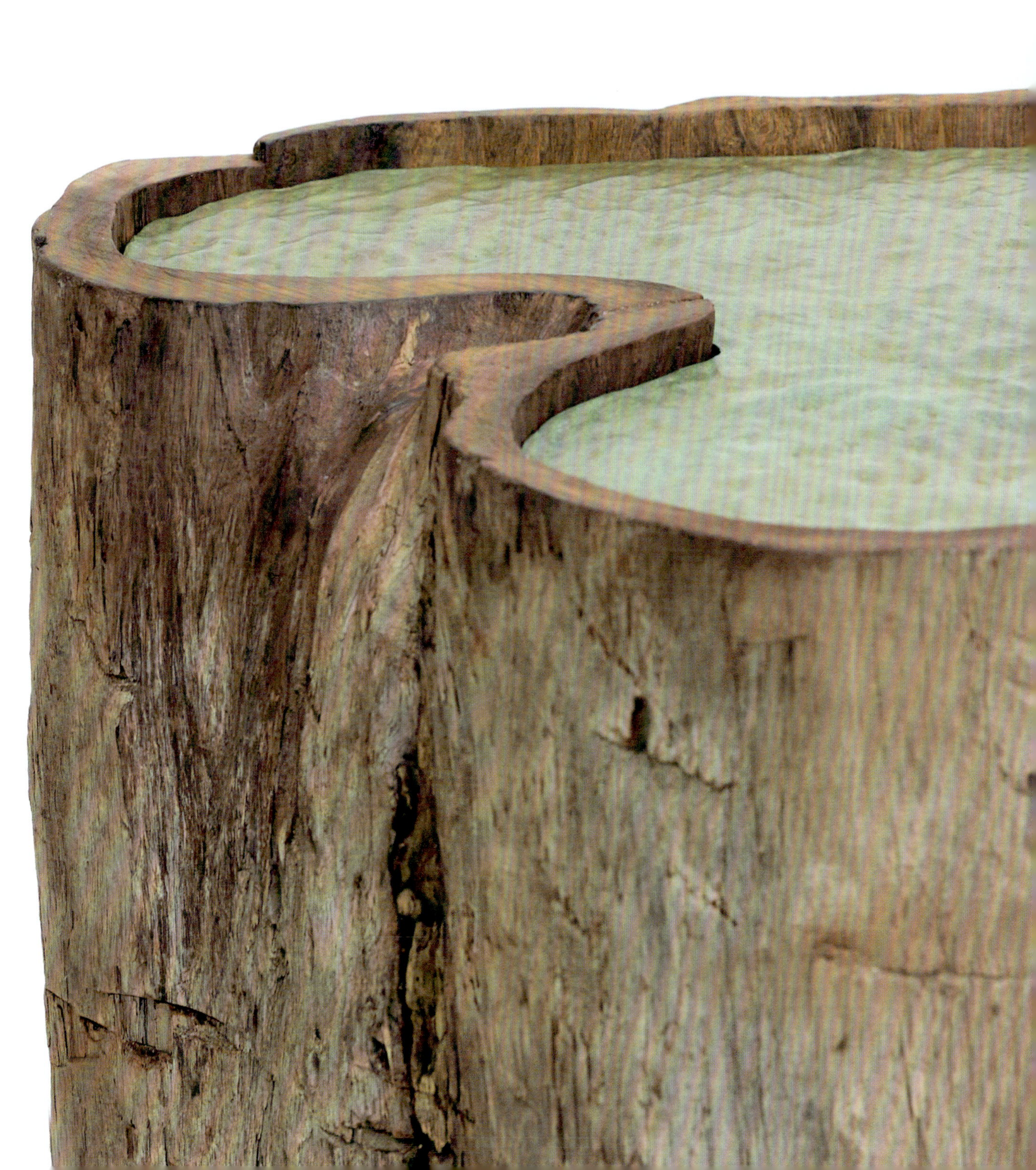

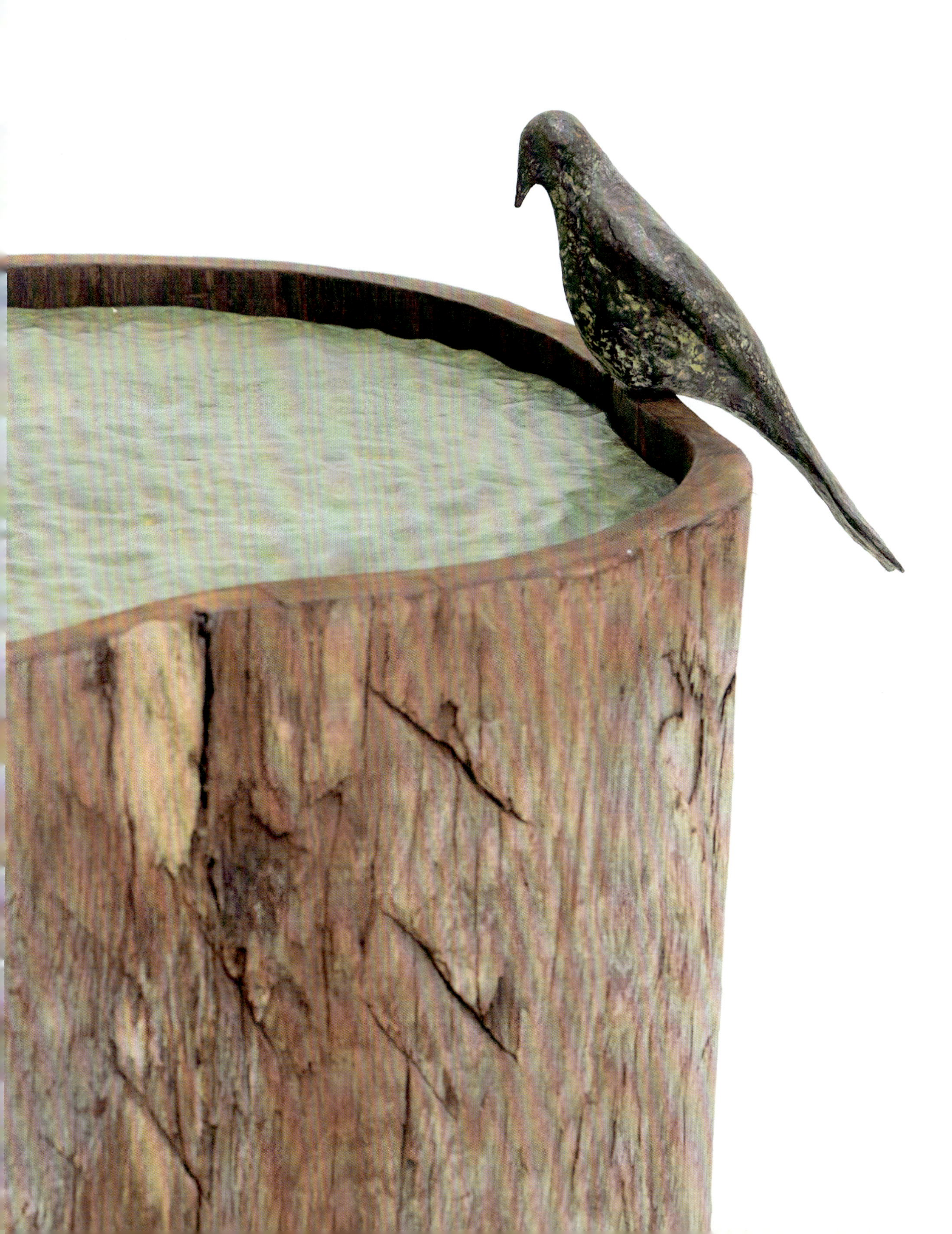

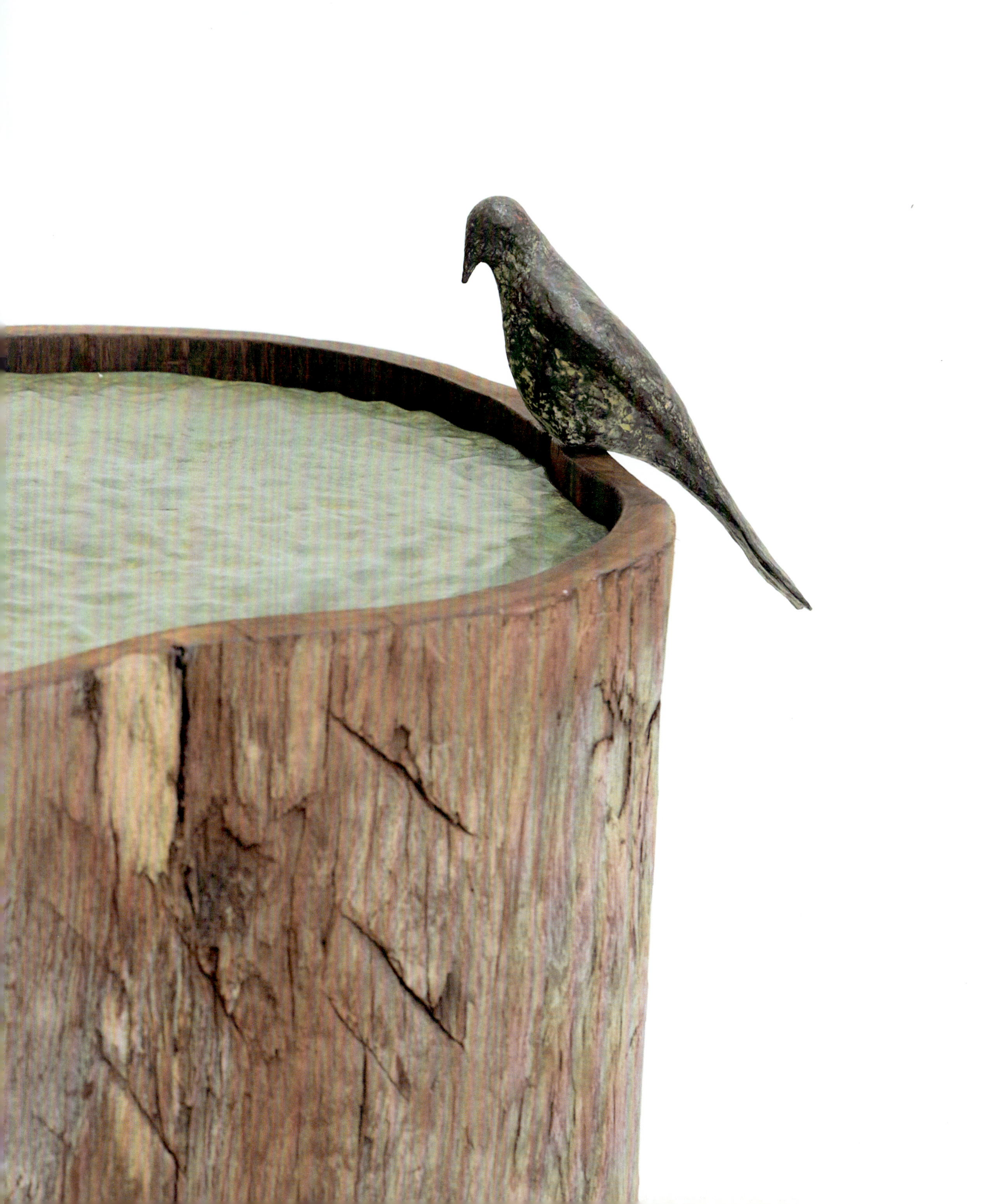

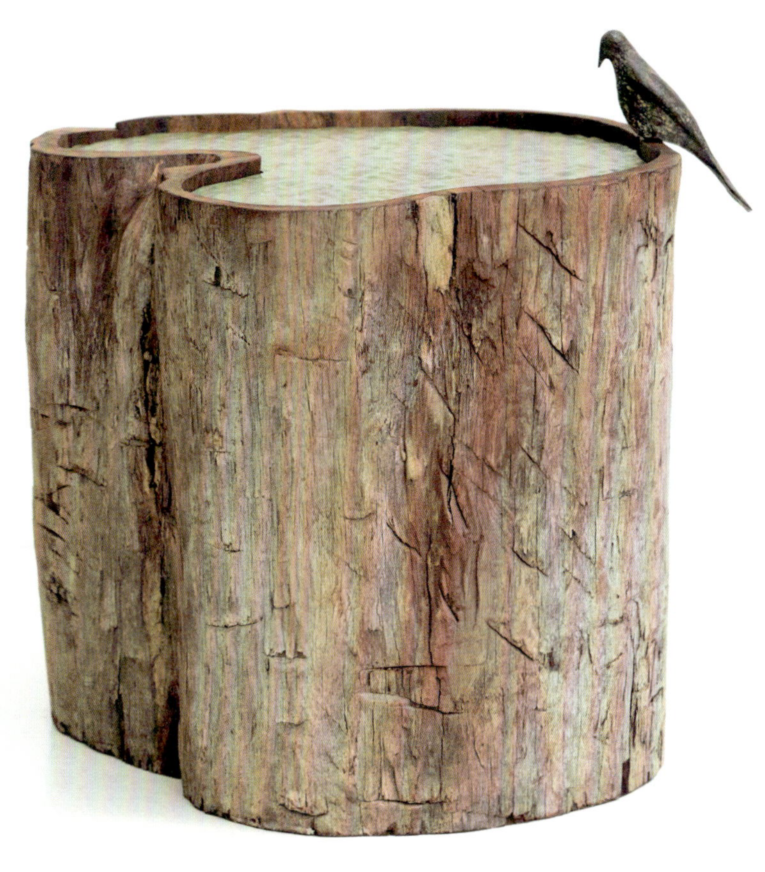

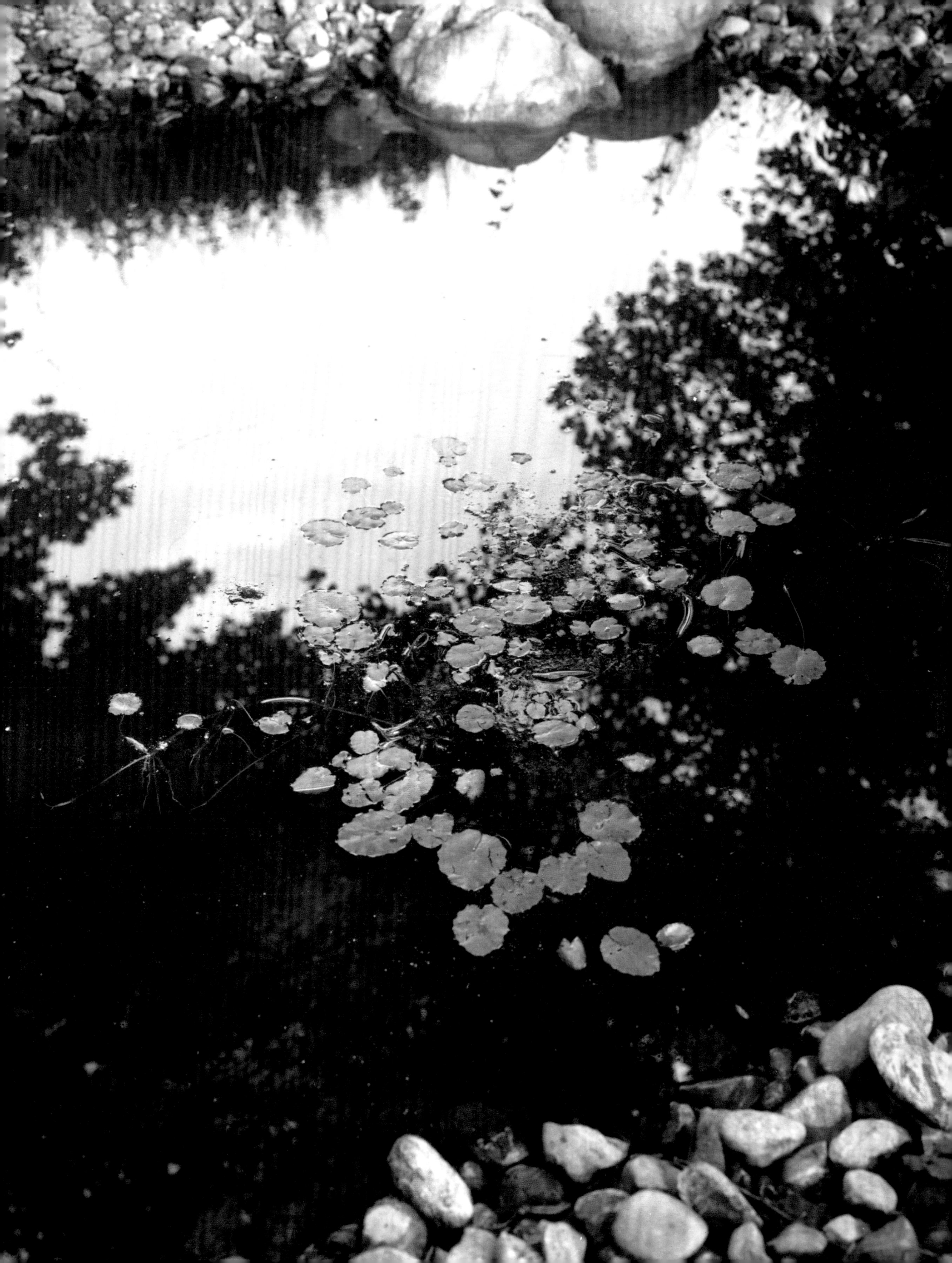

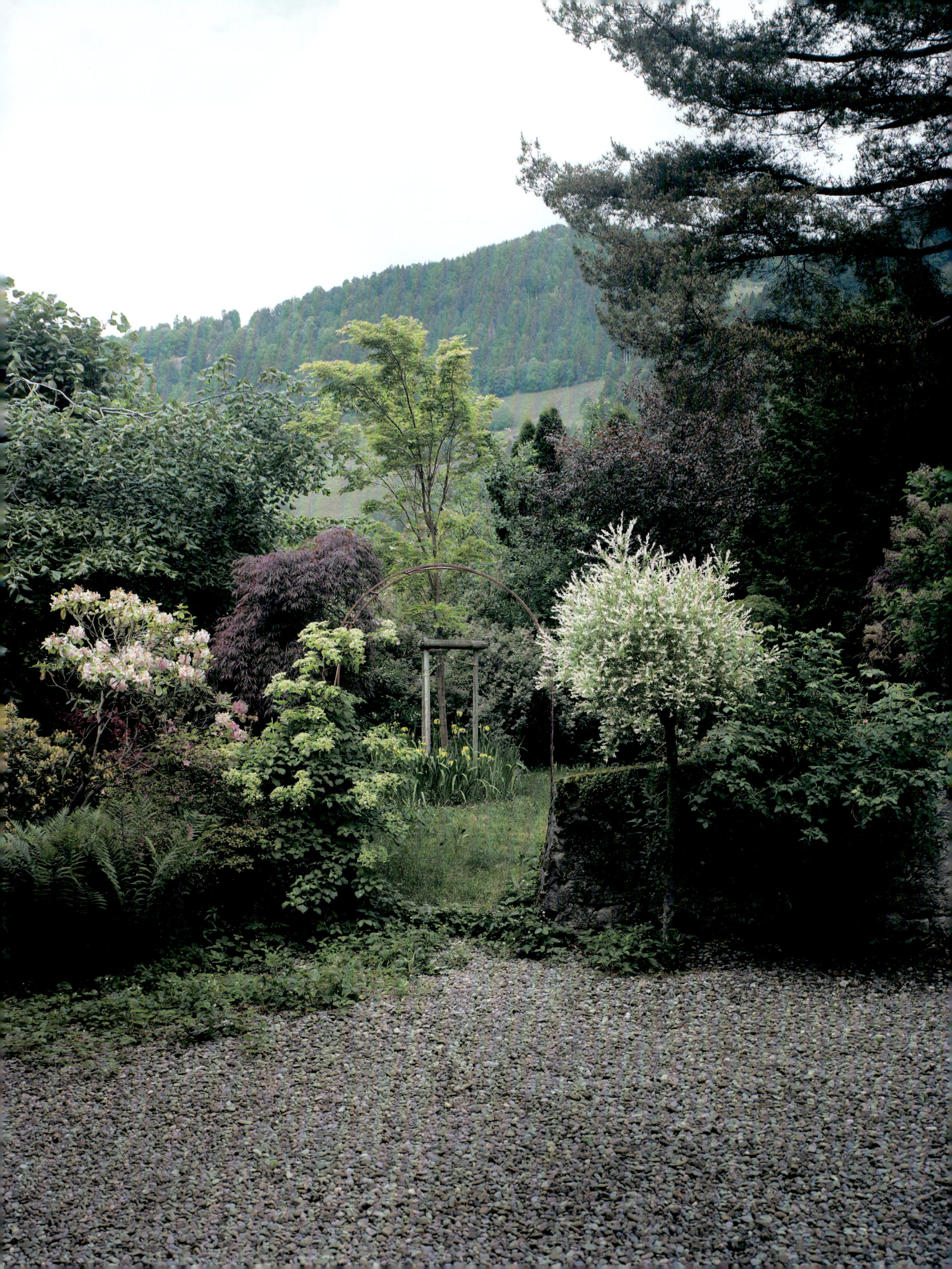

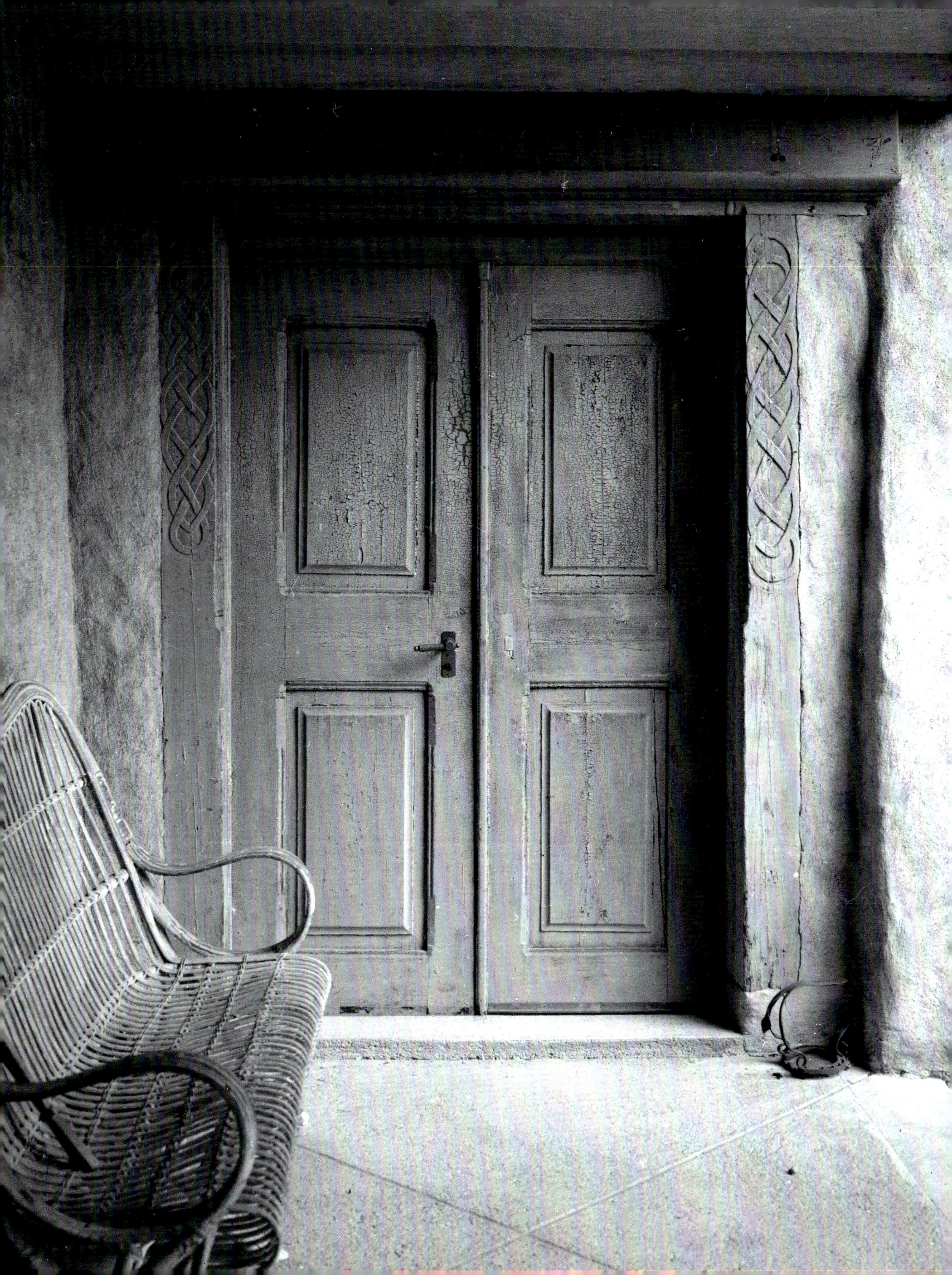

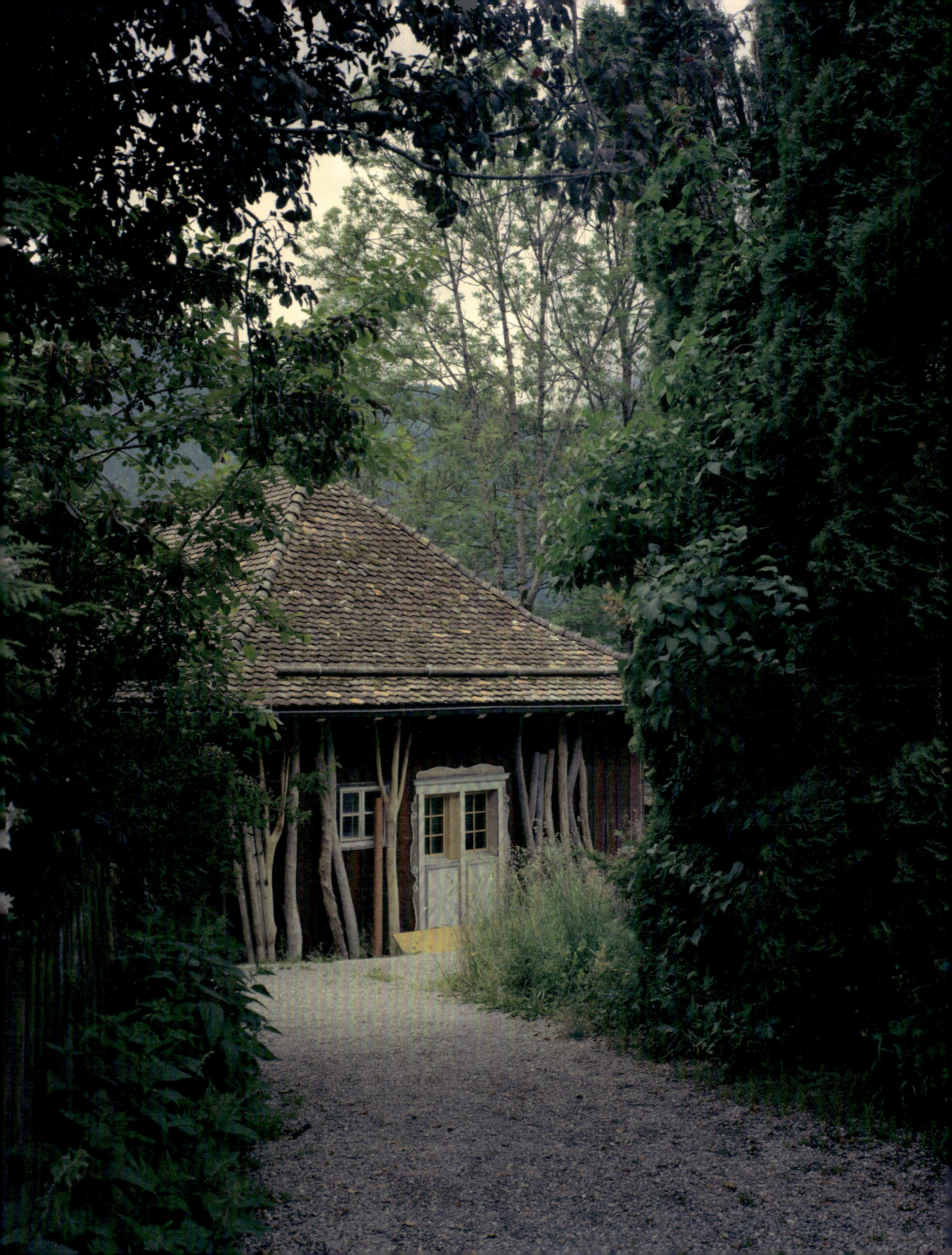

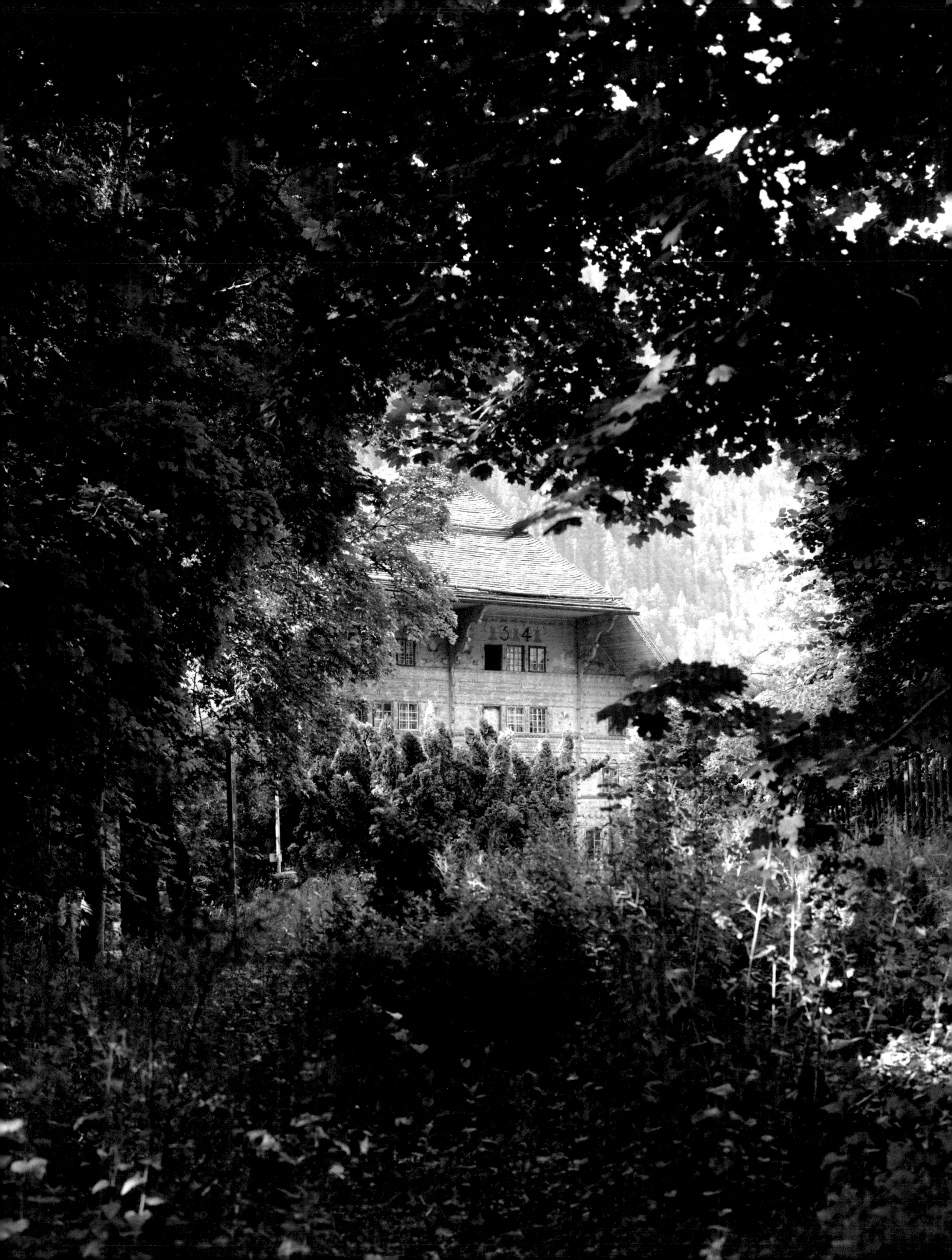

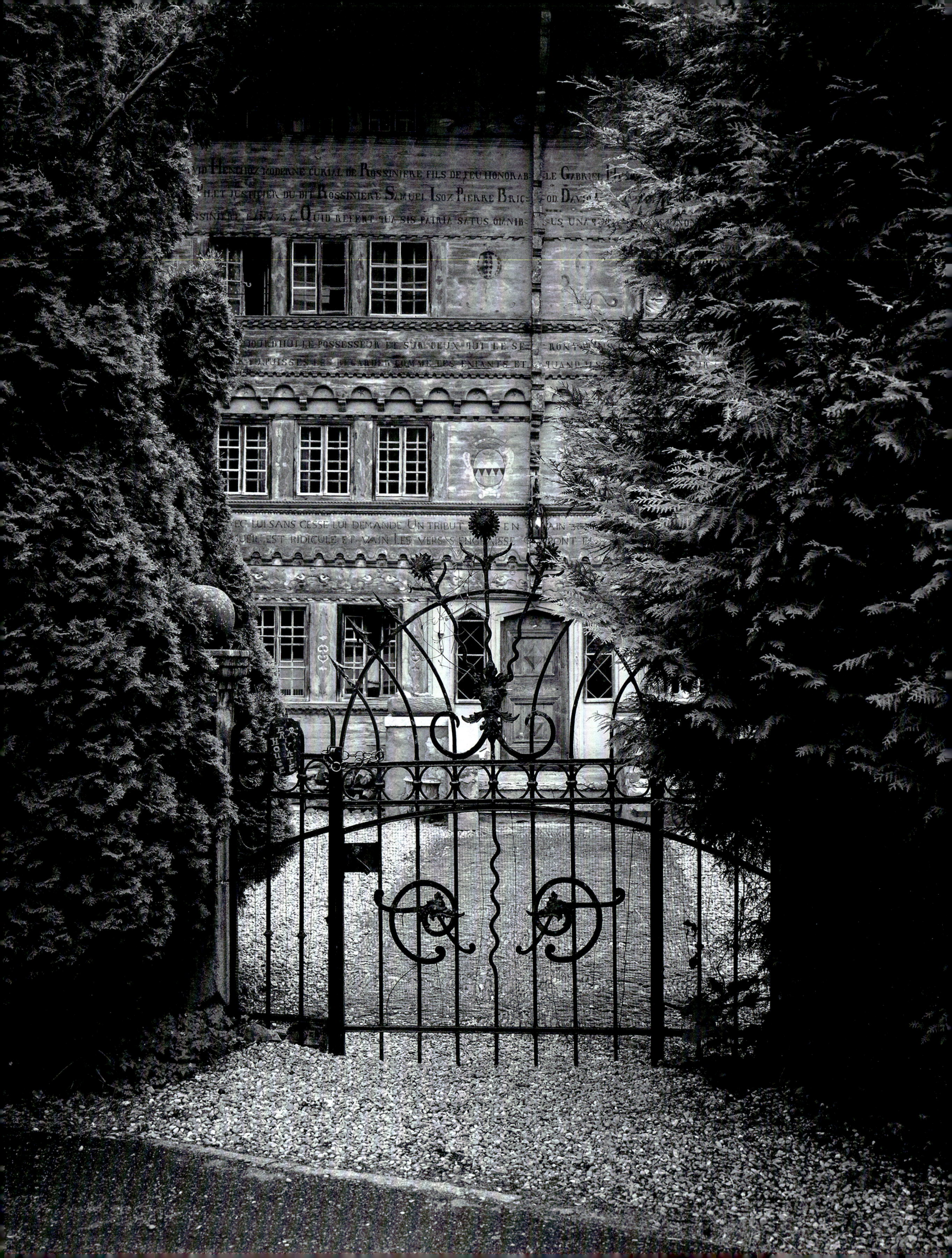
MODERNE CURIAL DE ROSSINIERE FILS DE FEU HONORAB LE GABRIEL
JUSTICIER DU DIT ROSSINIERE SAMUEL ISOZ PIERRE BRIC OD DAVID
QUID REFERT QUA SIS PATRIA SATUS OMNIB US UNA
SANS CESSE LUI DEMANDE UN TRIBUT
EST RIDICULE ET VAIN

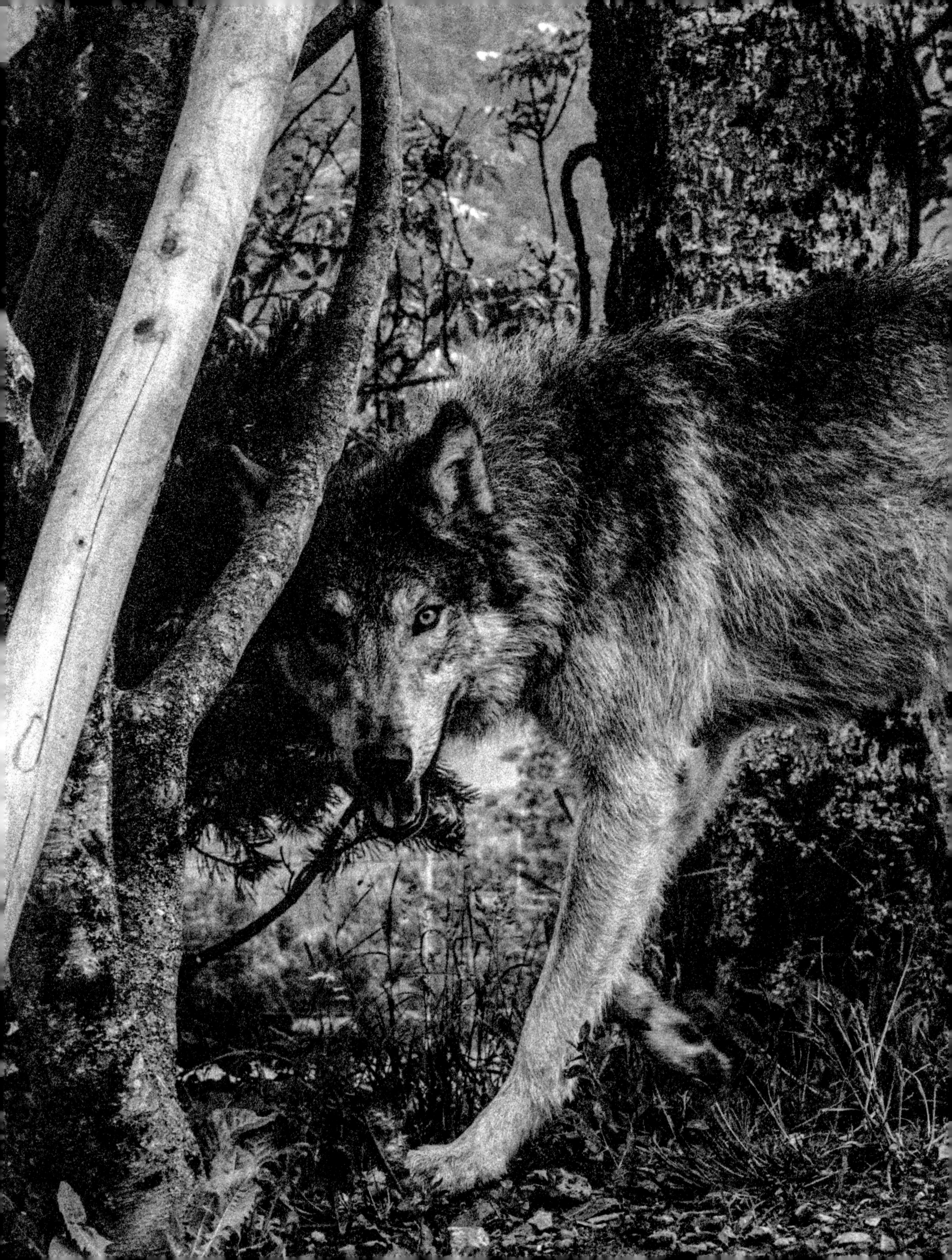

WORKS IN EXHIBITION

Bird on a Pond

2024

Rosewood and bronze
Unique
22 1/2 × 24 × 26 3/4 inches (57 × 61 × 68 cm)
Fonderie de Coubertin, Saint-Rémy-lès-Chevreuse, France

Skops

2024

Bronze
Edition 2/8, plus one artist's proof
9 7/8 × 4 inches (25 × 10 cm)
Fonderie de Coubertin, Saint-Rémy-lès-Chevreuse, France

Olive Tree with Owl

2024

Bronze
Edition 1/8, plus two artist's proofs
74 3/4 × 19 3/4 inches (190 × 50 cm)
Fonderie de Coubertin, Saint-Rémy-lès-Chevreuse, France

Chinook (Salmon)

2024

Bronze
Edition 1/8, plus two artist's proofs
11 × 31 1/2 × 4 3/4 inches (28 × 80 × 12 cm)
Fonderie de Coubertin, Saint-Rémy-lès-Chevreuse, France

Owl in Moonlight

2024

Bronze
Edition 2/8, plus two artist's proofs
72 7/8 × 12 5/8 × 12 5/8 inches (185 × 32 × 32 cm) (diameter at top)
Fonderie de Coubertin, Saint-Rémy-lès-Chevreuse, France

Small Tree with Owl

2024

Bronze
Edition 1/8 plus two artist's proofs
21 × 10 1/4 × 14 1/8 inches (53.5 × 26 × 36 cm)
Fonderie de Coubertin, Saint-Rémy-lès-Chevreuse, France

Sleeping Dove (Laying Bird)

2024

Alabaster and bronze
Edition 1/8, plus two artist's proofs
7 7/8 × 11 3/4 inches (20 × 30 cm)
Fonderie Patrick Laroche, Paris

Ame-no-kaku

2022

Bronze and gold leaf
Edition 2/8, plus two artist's proofs
81 1/8 × 76 × 16 7/8 inches (206 × 193 × 43 cm)
Fonderie de Coubertin, Saint-Rémy-lès-Chevreuse, France

Athene Noctua

2022

Bronze, fire gilded
Edition 5/8, plus four artist's proofs
$7\,^{7}/_{8} \times 6\,^{1}/_{4} \times 5\,^{7}/_{8}$ inches (20 × 16 × 15 cm)
Fonderie de Coubertin, Saint-Rémy-lès-Chevreuse, France

Wepwawet

2022

Bronze
Edition 2/8, plus two artist's proofs
$29\,^{1}/_{2} \times 11\,^{3}/_{4} \times 57\,^{1}/_{2}$ inches (75 × 30 × 146 cm)
Fonderie de Coubertin, Saint-Rémy-lès-Chevreuse, France

Daal

2022

Bronze and gold leaf
Edition 1/8, plus two artist's proofs
$59\,^{7}/_{8} \times 59\,^{7}/_{8} \times 14\,^{1}/_{8}$ inches (152 × 152 × 36 cm)
Fonderie de Coubertin, Saint-Rémy-lès-Chevreuse, France

Serpentes

2018

Bronze and platinum leaf
Edition 2/4, plus one artist's proof
$15\,^{3}/_{4} \times 9\,^{7}/_{8} \times 26\,^{3}/_{8}$ inches (40 × 25.1 × 67 cm)
Fonderie Patrick Laroche, Paris

Lakshmi

2022

Bronze, fire gilded
Artist's proof 3/4, from an edition of 8 plus four artist's proofs
$15\,^{3}/_{8} \times 5\,^{7}/_{8} \times 9$ inches (39 × 15 × 23 cm)
Fonderie de Coubertin, Saint-Rémy-lès-Chevreuse, France

Sobek

2018

Bronze and gold leaf
Edition 3/3, plus one artist's proof
$16\,^{7}/_{8} \times 21\,^{5}/_{8} \times 81\,^{1}/_{8}$ inches (43 × 55 × 206 cm)
Fonderie Patrick Laroche, Paris

Wood Pile / Misty Swamp

2022

Screen: sipo wood, platinum, palladium,
gold leaf, and oil paint
Unique
$88\,^{5}/_{8} \times 97\,^{5}/_{8} \times ^{3}/_{4}$ inches (225 × 248 × 2 cm)

BIOGRAPHY

Solo Exhibitions

2023

Hayawan, Robilant+Voena, Saint Moritz, Switzerland
Yakushima, the Mystic Island, Galerie Gastou, Paris
Hayawan, Robilant+Voena, New York

2022

Hayawan, Robilant+Voena, London

2019

Vestigae Naturae, "L'École des Arts Joailliers,"
Van Cleef & Arpels, Kyoto University, Kyoto, Japan

2018

Dialogue, "maison Valentino," Place Vendôme, Paris

2017

Retour d'Expédition, "L'École des Arts Joailliers,"
Van Cleef & Arpels, Paris

2015

Harumi Klossowska de Rola, Les Trois Pommes–Cabinet des arts,
Zurich, Switzerland

2011

Crânes, Galerie du Passage, Paris

Group Exhibitions

2022

Rara avis, White Cube, Paris

2019

Venetian art and life style experience, Chahan Gallery x Colnaghi,
Abbazia San Gregorio, Venice

2015

Cabana Pop Up Store, Mi Art Contemporary Art and Design Fair, Milan

2010

"*Cabinet Contemporain de Curiosités*" of Thomas Erber, Colette, Paris

2002

Creatività Riflessa, Palazzo Doria Pamphilj San Martino al Cimino, Viterbo, Italy
Harumi Klossowska x Donata Wenders, Grand Chalet, Rossinière, Switzerland
Harumi Klossowska x Donata Wenders, Tokyo

Collaborations

2024

Wes Anderson. Creation of an object

2022

Goossens. Creation of a collection of objects for Goosens, Paris

2018

Goossens. Creation of a collection of objects for Goosens, Paris

2017

Valentino. Creation of seven minaudières "the seven deadly sins"
for the fashion show Haute Couture

2016

Chopard. Creation of four new pieces "haute joaillerie" for Chopard
Valentino. Creation of several tiaras for the fashion show Haute Couture

2014

Creation of four pieces "haute joaillerie" for Chopard. Exhibition at Baselworld

2012

Chopard. Creation of three "haute joaillerie" pieces for Chopard

2008

Boucheron. Creation of two "haute joaillerie" pieces for Boucheron
Exhibition-sale at the "Salons Boucheron," Place Vendôme, Paris

Publications

2023

Harumi Klossowska. Yakushima, catalog, Galerie Gastou

2022

Harumi Klossowska de Rola. Hayawan, catalog, Robilant+Voena

2021

Harumi Klossowska de Rola, dir. art. Atelier Franck Durand

2021

Harumi Klossowska de Rola. Vestigia Naturae, catalog, École des Arts Joailliers
by Van Cleef & Arpels, Kyoto University, Kyoto, Japan

2017

Fauna: The Art of Jewelry, Patrick Mauriès and Évelyne Possémé,
Thames & Hudson

Collections

Musée des Arts décoratifs, Paris

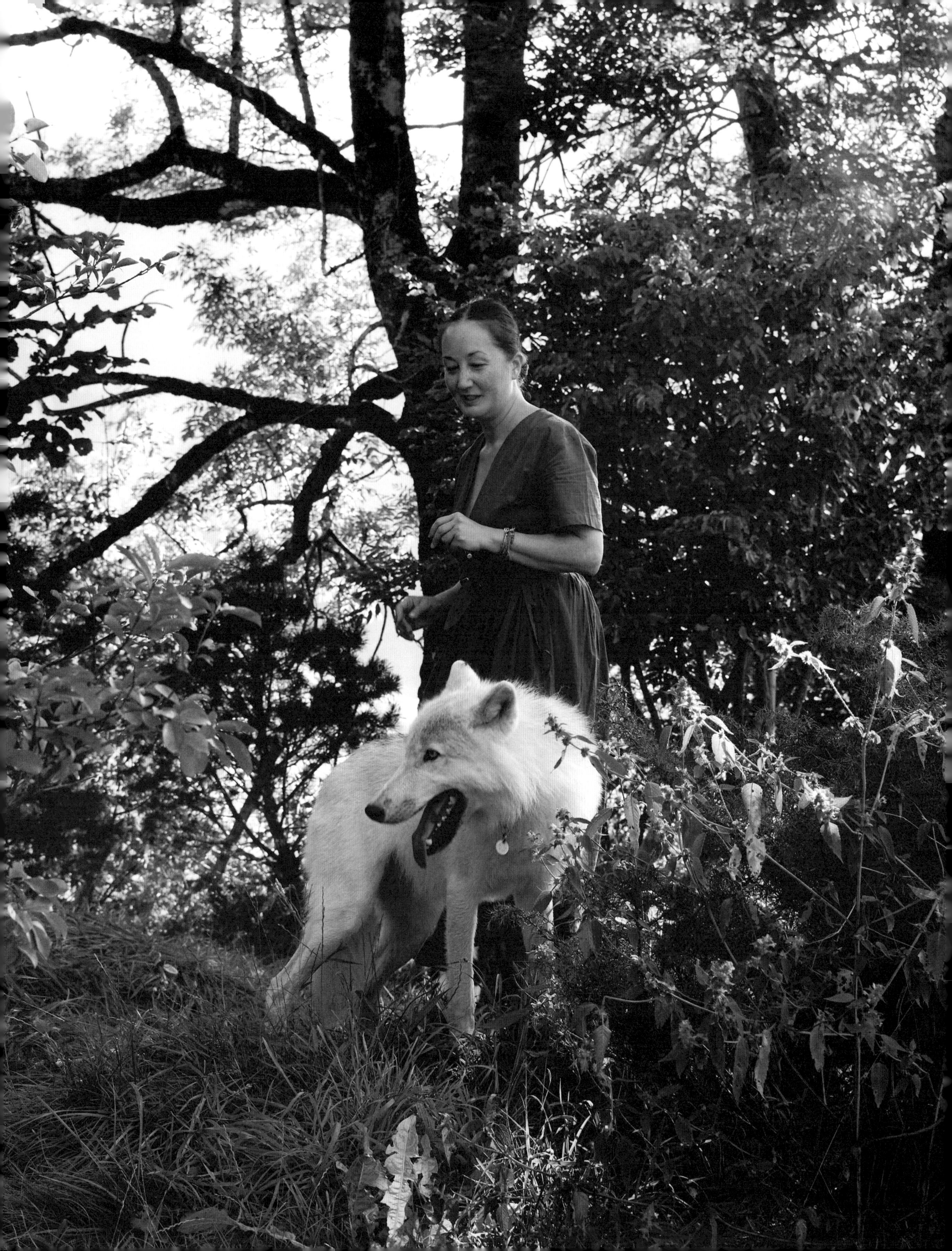

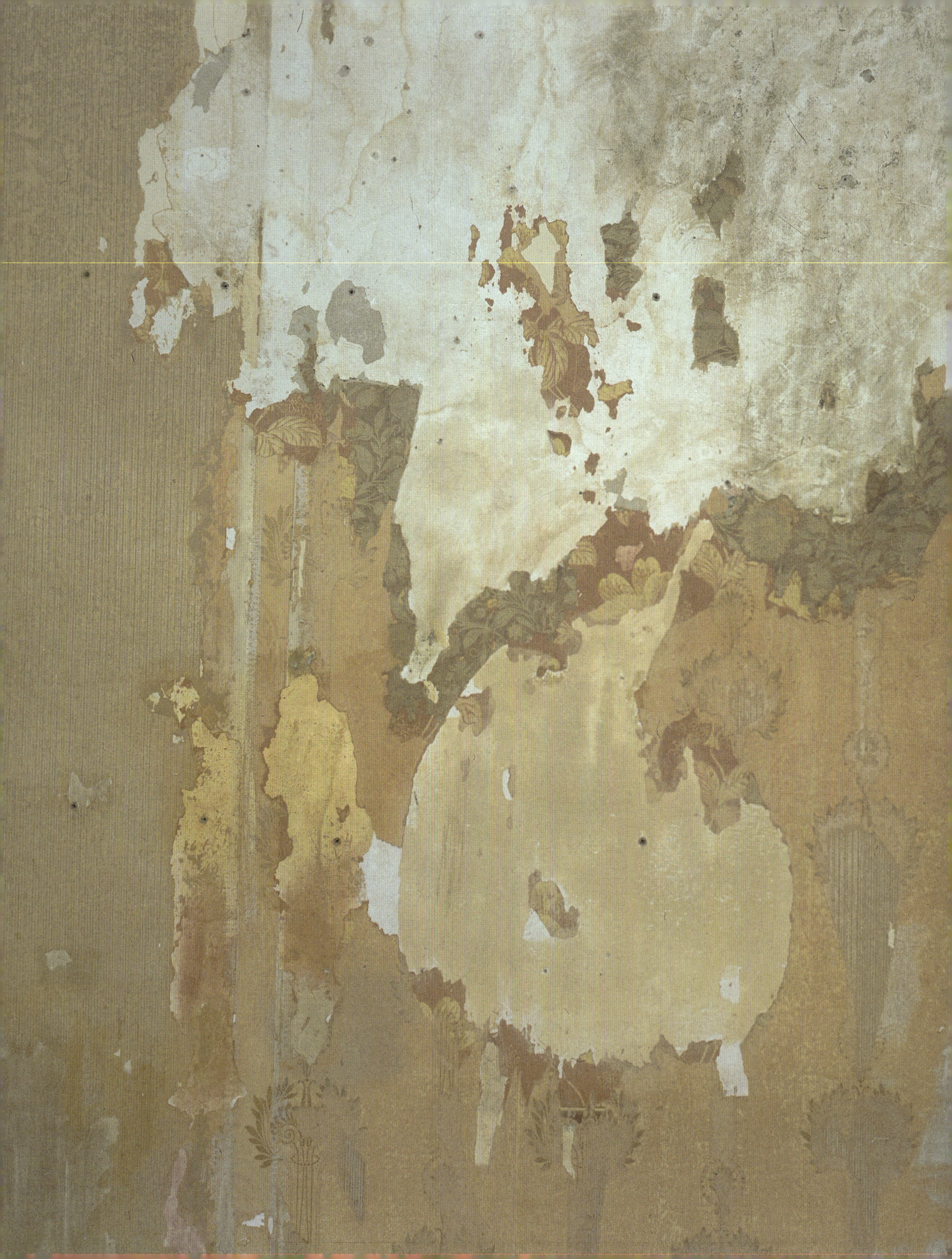